WHAT'S THAT WEED?

WHAT'S THAT WEED?

Know your weeds and learn to live with them

Guy Barter

CONTENTS

Introduction

What is a weed?   6
How do weeds grow?   8
How do weeds spread?   10
Managing weeds   14
Benefits for biodiversity   16

Annuals   18

Perennials   78

Woody   124

Glossary   134
Resources   136
Index   138
Acknowledgments   142

WHAT IS A WEED?

There is a revolution going on in the world of weeds. After decades when weeds seemed beaten by chemical herbicides, it turned out that the overuse of those herbicides led to resistant weeds, polluted water, and damaged ecosystems. It is now widely accepted that the concepts of the "war on weeds" and even "eradicating weeds" are outdated and highly questionable in the face of collapsing biodiversity. Consequently, the language associated with weed control is changing. Herbicides used to be given fearsome names such as "Commando" and "Missile," but now less assertive names are favored that will not encourage aggressive weed control. In research, weeds are sometimes referred to as "non-crop arable plants" or "cryptocrops," which are far less pejorative terms.

The aesthetic appreciation of weeds has changed, too. Wild plants are not all weeds, although all weeds (except invasive alien plants) are wild plants. Wild plants are now much more widely used in gardens for their simple beauty, rural connotations, and benefit to wildlife. Cow parsley, for example, an elegant wild plant without weedy tendencies, has previously been unwelcome in gardens but is now commonplace in wilder borders and plantings. The truly weedy ground elder is an insect-friendly ground cover plant, while ragwort and creeping buttercup add color to wilder lawns.

Many weeds also have ardent supporters of their gastronomic properties, for example, nettle soup, typical of more generous opinions now held about weeds. All the same, too effusive a welcome could lead to problems. Wise gardeners will set boundaries; seed shedding will be curtailed and *cordons sanitaires* of cultivated ground will confine perennial weeds to where they can be enjoyed without consequences.

An ecological definition

By tradition, weeds are defined as plants growing where they are not wanted, but there is more to it than that; they are plants that have an adverse effect on crops or ornamental plantings. In ecological terms, they are opportunists and

Weeds play a vital role in local ecosystems and have important benefits for wildlife.

survivors that fill niches created by human activities. Of the 370,000 or so plant species on Earth, just 3 percent can behave as weeds.

Unfortunately a few of these have proved particularly able to spread outside their native range, becoming global pests that are sometimes termed "invasive aliens." The sale and distribution of invasive nonnative plants are often controlled by legislation. In the US, see the USDA Federal Noxious Weed List (p.136). Native weeds, however, often bring benefits for wildlife and ecosystems, but from a gardening point of view, they need to be managed in a cost-effective and practical way while avoiding harming, and if possible actively enhancing, wildlife and the environment.

Recognizing individual weeds and understanding their life cycles, their favored ecological niches, and their strategies to survive, is essential to managing weed populations. This book aims to help gardeners take the first steps in managing weeds in a way that will reduce work and expense, and support wildlife, without sacrificing any of the benefits of gardening.

Management techniques

Weeds play a vital role in local ecosystems, and have important benefits for wildlife that we need to bear in mind before we start controlling them. Managing weeds to keep populations low remains important to protect valued plants and structures. However, this involves taking a broader view

and using a range of weeding techniques that include clearing ground before planting, stale seedbeds (p.135) to diminish initial weed "pressure," mulches, hoeing, hand-weeding, and targeting weeds before they become established. Combining these is called "integrated weed management"—a series of minor measures add up to give good results for the least effort to gardeners and the environment.

As the importance of sustainability and biodiversity increases, gardening societies have revised their advice and practices on weed management to take a more relaxed view of weeds. Gardeners are encouraged to be biodiversity net positive, because greater plant diversity will support increased invertebrate communities. Gardening helps keep the balance between the weeds and the plants you want to grow, to create visual harmony and a productive plot.

As a result, lighter-touch weed management is now standard. Annual trimming, for example, replaces total herbicides that leave bare soil; adding more grass seed to out-compete lawn weeds (overseeding) is used to keep lawn weeds to an acceptable level while avoiding selective herbicides; and summer-sown cover crops (green manures) prevent weeds from flourishing on bare soil over winter, replacing repeated cultivation that damages soil and biodiversity.

HOW DO WEEDS GROW?

When you see a weed, the most useful thought to have is, "Why is that plant growing there?" Once you know why, and how that weed takes advantage of the opportunities you have provided, you are well on the way to managing it.

Annual weeds probably evolved to exploit opportunities such as the retreat of glaciers or the collapse of cliffs and riverbanks. They produce numerous, easily spread seeds to colonize fleeting areas of bare ground, of which gardeners provide many opportunities during cultivation.

Perennial weeds have extremely robust structures such as persistent bulbils (small bulbs or bulblike growths) or rhizomes that embed themselves among perennial garden plants, becoming hard to target and control. They probably evolved in highly competitive environments such as forests or scrub where they had to survive fierce competition with larger plants or depredation from browsing animals. These weeds are vulnerable in cultivated ground that is tilled every year, while annual weeds find it hard to persist in unmoved soil where their seeds lie, unburied, on the surface and their numbers are depleted by birds and insects. Burial induces dormancy in many weed seeds and the dormant seeds, often in great numbers, persist for years in the soil, forming a "seed bank."

Seed banks are a crucial part of weed biology. Every long-cultivated garden will have seeds in the whole cultivated depth of soil. These seeds decline, sometimes quickly, often slowly, over the years. Whenever the soil is cultivated afresh, seeds are brought to the surface, where a proportion germinate to begin the cycle again. They are very specific in what causes them to germinate, which is often light—if they can "sense" light they "know" they are near the surface. The same goes for fluctuating temperatures.

Similarly, a bud bank persists where perennial weeds thrive. Buried bulbs, rhizomes, and root fragments persist and, when control is eased, provide the basis for a rapid resurgence of weeds.

Whenever the soil is cultivated afresh, seeds are brought to the surface where a proportion germinate.

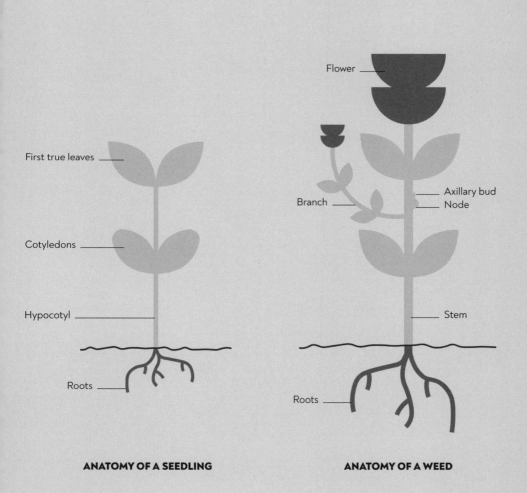

First true leaves

Cotyledons

Hypocotyl

Roots

ANATOMY OF A SEEDLING

Flower

Branch

Axillary bud

Node

Stem

Roots

ANATOMY OF A WEED

HOW DO WEEDS SPREAD?

Weeds are adept at short-range dispersal via wind (groundsel, for example, p.64) or explosive seed pods (such as hairy bitter cress, p.32). Annual weeds produce enormous numbers of seeds—a large, overlooked groundsel plant may produce 25,000 seeds, although 1,500 is more usual. Numerous seeds are necessarily small seeds. They can travel on the wind, on tools and clothing, and among crop seeds. Such small seeds cannot emerge from a soil depth greater than 2in (5cm), so mulches, shallow hoeing, and stale seedbeds (p.135) are effective.

Many weeds, including groundsel, have hairs that enhance wind dispersal, while others, for example cleavers (p.44), have sticky seeds that adhere to clothing, feathers, or fur. Cleavers avoid the common weed strategy of having numerous tiny seeds, instead producing fewer (350 per plant), bigger seeds. These produce stronger, more competitive seedlings and can emerge from deeper in the soil than tiny seeds.

Perennial weeds can be spread by seeds, for example dandelions (p.120), or by flooding, as with Japanese knotweed (p.114), but in the yard their spread is usually by root fragments. These may come from imported soil, or new plant pots, while some may travel within the yard on tools and boots. While fragments are much less numerous than seeds, they give rise to bigger weed plants with ample resources to quickly embed themselves.

International weed spread

Continents and oceans prove no barrier to weeds. Seeds used in agriculture have historically been a potent means of travel for associated weeds. Modern

Many weeds have hairs that enhance wind dispersal, while other have sticky seeds that adhere to clothes or fur.

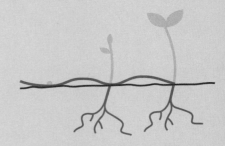

Rhizomes A rhizome is a modified stem growing from a bud, first downward, then laterally, and finally upward, with a new shoot.

Stolons A stolon is a horizontal stem that develops from a bud and remains above ground, where it forms new plants.

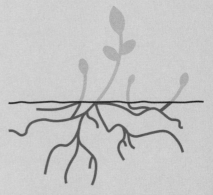

Seeds A seed contains all the material needed for a new plant to take root elsewhere. Seeds have many means of dispersal.

Spreading roots When root fragments are imported to gardens they introduce new plants that can spread rapidly.

seed-cleaning machinery, as well as efficient weed control, have reduced the weed burden of commercial seeds. Legislation to ensure high-quality seed is a cornerstone of modern plant production.

Trade, too, carries weeds around the world. Until modern times, weeds from far shores often sprouted up around wool mills, brought on imported fleeces, while ship's ballast of sand, soil, and gravel discarded at a jetty prior to taking on cargo, was also a noted source of weeds such as ragweed (p.26) and jimson weed (p.38). Modern transportation offers fewer opportunities for weed spread, as strict rules limit contamination with soil or vegetable materials.

One of the few modern routes for the introduction of potential weed species by trade is in bird food. These seeds are often the waste grains of farm crops and include weed seeds imported from other countries. Niger seeds (*Guizotia abyssinica*) from Africa and Asia, valued for feeding finches, have been found to contain over 100 different species, even though the product sold to gardeners is 99 percent pure.

Weed spread within gardens

However, by far the most common route for the spread of weeds is via plants, on garden machinery, and by gardeners. Some weeds, such as ground elder (p.86), have herbal uses and unwary gardeners no doubt contributed to its spread. Others arrive via gardens containing plants sourced worldwide. *Galinsoga parviflora* (p.42) is reputed to have gained entry to the UK via the Royal Botanic Gardens, Kew, apparently originally being grown as an interesting alpine plant. Himalayan balsam (p.46) and Japanese knotweed (p.114) were originally, albeit briefly, valued ornamental garden plants. Containerized plants are often infested with wood sorrel (p.54) and hairy bitter cress (p.32).

This process is ongoing, with apparently innocuous garden plants becoming invasive in the wild. Western skunk cabbage (*Lysichiton americanus*), a dramatic bog garden plant, has spread far beyond its native habitat in the wet areas of the Pacific Northwest and become a menace, proliferating in ditches and streams. The USDA lists 175 noxious weed species, mostly garden or aquarium plants, whose sale and cultivation are controlled. Gardeners are urged never to allow garden plants to spread into uncultivated areas.

Over the longer-term, alternating years of perennial planting with years of annual cropping presents weeds with fresh challenges.

Understanding plant life cycles

Each agricultural crop has its own associated weed population. Winter grains such as wheat are plagued by blackgrass (*Alopecurus myosuroides*), a weed that germinates in the fall and sheds seed around harvest time the following year.

The same applies to garden plants; vegetables are sown each spring in fertile soil, which favors seeds that germinate in spring, especially in the presence of nitrates (plant food)—including annual nettles (p.74) and white goosefoot (p.34). But fall sowing and pre-sowing cultivation means that overwintered and perennial weeds can be eradicated. Whereas with annual weeds, dormant seeds await the next spring-sown crop before germinating.

Overwintering weeds such as red dead-nettle (p.50), chickweed (p.70), and annual bluegrass (p.60) grow wel among fall-sown crops, for example fava beans and shallots, or perennial plantings that have open unshaded areas, herbaceous perennials, strawberries, roses, and asparagus. Mulching to prevent them saves much laborious spring weeding.

Perennial plantings provide "cover" for perennial weeds. Likely sites include soft fruit, shrubberies, hedges, and "prairie" type plantings. These typically harbor couch grass (p.96), hedge bindweed (p.92), and ground elder (p.86). Hedge bindweed is brilliantly adapted to clambering over taller plants; ground elder has deep green leaves that can photosynthesize under hedges; while couch grass has questing rhizomes that can swiftly spread. Being intertwined in other vegetation, these weeds are exceptionally difficult to remove, and they limit the useful lifetimes of perennial plantings.

Over the longer term, alternating years of perennial planting followed by years of annual cropping presents weeds with fresh challenges and reduces their number. Or, intractable areas can be sown to grass and weeds eradicated by the mower.

Lawns are a special case. They mimic the dense sward produced where sheep or rabbits are numerous. The mower blades are less discriminating than grazing animals, so spiny plants such as thistles (p.68, p.94) are eradicated by the mower. Other weeds that form rosettes close to the soil are challenging for both mowers and grazing animals (such as daisies, p.90), while sprawling weeds such as clover and speedwell (p.76) avoid mowing and quickly regrow. Lawn weeds can be suppressed by promoting grass growth, hoeing them, or in extreme cases selective herbicides that spare grass but kill broad-leaved weeds. However, lawn growth can be damaged by foot traffic and the same opportunists found in annual crops—annual bluegrass (p.60) and chickweed (p.70)—can exploit any bare, worn patches until the grass can be restored.

MANAGING WEEDS

To manage weeds, identifying them and understanding their life cycle, persistence, and potential for spread are crucial. Knowing that they may have redeeming features such as value to wildlife means that ideally, the modern gardener exercises tolerance where benefits are to be found.

Annual weeds can be managed by preventing seeds being shed, at all costs. If they are shed they should not be buried as many will become dormant below the soil surface, sometimes persisting for decades, ready to germinate after digging. Such is the enormity of weed seed production that more than 95 percent of annual weeds have to be prevented from seeding just to avoid an infestation worsening.

Perennial weeds must be entirely eliminated, leaving no roots or bulbils. This often requires repeated digging out over several years or, in severe cases, a fallow period for at least one growing season where the soil is left bare so any surviving weed plantlets can be identified and carefully dug out before replanting with perennial garden plants.

Total weed elimination is unrealistic; the best that gardeners can reasonably expect is weed management, where you shift the ecology of the garden to be unfavorable to weeds so their numbers remain at an acceptable level of infestation. This level can be high in, say, a wildlife lawn, or very low, as in an immaculate vegetable garden. It is up to the gardener to decide their level of tolerance and try to achieve this while doing a minimum of environmental harm.

Shift the ecology of the garden to be unfavorable to weeds so their numbers remain at an acceptable level.

BENEFITS FOR BIODIVERSITY

Weeds, even if left to set seed, seldom compare with trees and ponds for wildlife benefit, but they can make a contribution to a garden's overall environmental benefit. Massive seed production means abundant flowers, and annual weeds are often highly beneficial to insects seeking pollen and nectar. Seeds support birds and insects, but can be risky except in "wild" gardens, as allowing the plants to seed can lead to subsequent infestations.

Bare soil, particularly in wet weather, often in the fall, is quickly colonized by annual weeds, either from the seed bank or from seeds newly arrived in the garden. However, the weed "carpet" protects the soil, while scavenging plant nutrients that would otherwise be washed away by heavy rain, and the foliage feeds wildlife. The weeds subsequently return the nutrients to the garden plants after they are dug in or added to the compost piles.

Perennial weeds, with their uncanny ability to insinuate themselves into hedge bases, amid shrubs, and in unused areas, can be considered a kind of "guerrilla ground cover." They bring sustenance and protection for wildlife in areas gardeners cannot easily tend, and so earn their place. Clovers and other lawn "weeds" bring many benefits to wildlife, as do stands of nettles, for example around compost piles, or brambles in less conspicuous hedges. Too often these are subjected to repeated spraying or excessive trimming, degrading valuable mini-habitats where a more relaxed approach supports garden wildlife.

So, with today's more environmentally conscious approach to horticulture, the idea of blitzing all weeds in the quest for an immaculate garden should become a thing of the past. In the urgent need to repair degraded areas and protect pollinators, home gardeners can play their part by appreciating that weeds have their value and simply letting some of them be.

Clovers and other lawn "weeds" bring many benefits to wildlife, as do nettles around compost piles.

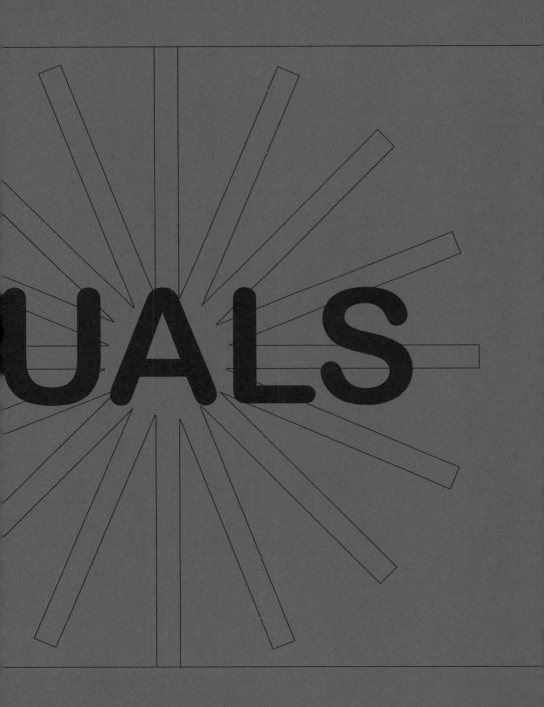

WHAT IS AN ANNUAL WEED?

Annual plants complete their entire life cycle in one growing season. This starts when it is warm enough for seeds to germinate and plants to grow, and it ends when cold winter weather brings growth to an end. Annual life cycles are effective strategies for weeds in many garden situations, notably vegetable gardens and flowerbeds that are planted for each season. They are less advantaged in perennial crops or plantings where opportunities for their numerous seeds to find and exploit a gap are limited.

Annuals with very short life cycles are sometimes called ephemerals. Strictly speaking, this means just one day, but it is used loosely here to indicate several generations per year. Annual bluegrass (p.60) and groundsel (p.64) have very short life cycles and thrive in areas where opportunities are fleeting, such as plant nurseries, propagation areas, and gaps in paving. The downside of being an ephemeral is that the mature plants are small, so can only produce limited numbers of seeds.

Weeds, being great survivors, keep their options open. Many annuals can germinate in the fall, cling to life over winter, and flourish in spring. These overwintering annuals, such as red dead-nettle (p.50), can grow into luxuriant plants in spring and produce masses of seeds, many of which will lie dormant all summer until they start the cycle again in the fall. Dormancy is a key feature of many annual weed seeds.

Overwintering annuals are very successful in agriculture, where most crops are sown in the fall. They can thrive in gardens where open perennial plantings leave them space to survive winters. Cleavers (p.44) are an example, where the large overwintered plant produces a heavier crop of its large seeds.

Many annuals can germinate in the fall, cling to life over winter, and flourish in spring.

GARLIC

Alliaria petiolata

Jack-by-the-hedge

Size 8–48 in (20–120 cm)

Spread 4–8 in (10–20 cm)

Seeds Late summer, 20 seeds per flower

Germinates Late winter, spring

Where it grows Hedges, open ground, and gardens

Garlic mustard can be alarmingly abundant in fertile, moist, shady places, often colonizing less cultivated parts of gardens such as rockeries and shrub borders. In North America, where it is not native, it was unwisely introduced as a potherb and medicine. A biennial plant that overwinters as a rosette, it is now considered a noxious weed with rampant spread that suppresses native vegetation, particularly in the understory of woods as it tolerates some shade. Experts advise eliminating it by pulling it out before it can set seed.

The garlic-scented, triangular leaves make recognition easy. Up to 30 white flowers with the typical four petals of the cabbage family are carried on each stalk, followed by elongated seed pods. In North America, similar plants have divided (compound) leaves rather than the simple (undivided) ones of garlic mustard, and include cut-leaf toothwort (*Cardamine concatenata*), which also has white brassica flowers.

Management
Preventing seed set is key to management. The tiny, wind-dispersed seeds remain viable for five years or more, but this plant cannot stand competition from dense plantings nor cultivation and hoeing. It is easily hand-pulled, with no regeneration from the roots.

MUSTARD

ABOVE Garlic mustard overwinters as a ground-level rosette of scalloped, heart-shaped leaves.

ABOVE RIGHT Typical brassica family flowers are followed by seed pods.

RIGHT Garlic mustard is vigorous in growth and will quickly colonize areas of the garden.

COMMON

Ambrosia artemisiifolia

Annual ragweed, small ragweed

Height 2–6 ft (60–180 cm)

Spread 12–24 in (30–60 cm)

Seeds Late summer, early fall, 3,500 per plant

Germinates Spring

Where it grows Fertile cultivated soils, especially near bird feeders

This North American native also occurs in other regions, spreading by its numerous seeds, which can lie dormant in the soil for up to 40 years. Chilling and light are needed for the seeds to germinate. In the UK, it occurs as a rare contaminant of imported wild bird seed, but does not persist, although it is established in France.

Tall, branched, almost shrublike, with fernlike leaves, ragweed is highly competitive with garden plants. The abundant wind-borne pollen that the green flowers produce causes great discomfort to people suffering from allergies. Western ragweed (*Ambrosia psilostachya*), a tap-rooted perennial, and the European native mugwort (*Artemisia vulgaris*), also a perennial, with silvery-white hairs beneath the leaves, are similar plants.

Management
Preventing seed production is essential, either by hoeing or hand-weeding. Even small plants—such as those left after mowing or partially suppressed by foliage of taller plants including flowers and vegetables—can set seed. Mulching will prevent seeds germinating; they become dormant if buried, only to germinate when uncovered by subsequent cultivation. Under no-dig regimens (p.135), the seeds either germinate and can be hoed or are eaten by wildlife.

RAGWEED

TOP Seedlings of common ragweed appear in spring and grow rapidly.

ABOVE The stems and compound leaves are hairy, and the latter are divided into numerous segments.

RIGHT Male flowers are produced at the stem tips, with female flowers lower on the plant.

SCARLET

Anagallis arvensis

Poor man's barometer

Height 3–12 in (8–30 cm)

Spread 2–20 in (5–50 cm)

Seeds Summer, fall,
900 per plant

Germinates Spring, summer

Where it grows Cultivated
and open ground, particularly
where the soil is sandy or chalky

This delicate, sprawling annual plant has angled stems; small, glossy leaves; and summer flowers that are usually red but may be blue or pink and are attractive to pollinators. It can overwinter as a green plant that flowers early, leading to a second generation before fall. Scarlet pimpernel is intolerant of shade, and the flowers open fully only in bright light, closing again in overcast conditions, hence the alternate common name "poor man's barometer." Common chickweed (p.70) is a similar plant. Scarlet pimpernel is poisonous to people, pets, and livestock.

Management
Seeds require light to germinate, so eliminating the first flush of weeds with a stale seedbed (p.135) gives good control. Hoeing, mulching, and hand-weeding are also effective. Because seed can remain viable for 10 years or more, preventing seeding is essential. However, scarlet pimpernel is a cheerful little plant and not very competitive under most circumstances. Except in crops sown in early spring—such as carrots and larkspur—it can often be tolerated and enjoyed for its charming, tiny flowers.

PIMPERNEL

ABOVE The small, shiny, dark green cotyledons (p.9) are at ground level. Triangular true leaves, spotted beneath, follow them.

LEFT The straggly stems are clothed with small, glossy leaves that grow in pairs and bear tiny red or pink, occasionally blue, flowers.

SHEPHERD'S

Capsella bursa-pastoris

Height 3–18 in (8–45 cm)

Spread 2–6 in (5–15 cm)

Seeds Summer, 5,000 per plant

Germinates All year round, but peaks in spring

Where it grows Well-drained, fertile soils

This highly variable, upright annual forms a basal rosette from which many stems arise, bearing tiny white flowers in the characteristic four-petaled configuration of cabbage family plants. The seeds, nectar, and foliage all provide food for wildlife.

Some shepherd's purse seeds show myxospermy, where a gelatinous layer forms around a seed when it gets wet. This modifies the area around the seed to hold more water and enhance seed-soil contact, valuable properties where adverse soil conditions occur. The seeds have also been shown to attract and kill nematodes, some of which are very damaging to plants. This makes shepherd's purse technically carnivorous. It self-pollinates and this results in innumerable, slightly different microspecies. The seedlings resemble those of many other plants, especially poppies.

Management
Mulching to prevent germination, repeated hoeing, and ultimately hand-pulling prevents seed shedding, which is essential to manage this weed. Stale seedbeds (p.135) are also effective.

PURSE

TOP The cotyledons are smooth and oval, carried on a short stalk. The initial true leaves are elongated and pointed, with a smooth or slightly toothed edge; subsequent leaves are deeply indented.

RIGHT Several flower stalks arise from a rosette of deeply lobed silvery-green leaves. Tiny white flowers are borne along the entire length of the stem, opening in succession from the base.

ABOVE Heart-shaped seed pods follow, releasing minuscule seeds that persist in the soil for at least five years.

HAIRY

Cardamine hirsuta

Popping cress, flickweed

Height 2–6 in (5–15 cm)

Spread 2–6 in (5–15 cm)

Seeds Late spring, summer, fall, early winter, 600 per plant

Germinates Spring and fall

Where it grows Any bare soil or potting mix

This tiny annual or biennial weed grows as small, dark green rosettes and once it has flowered it quickly sets seed pods that explode when mature, throwing seeds up to 3 ft (1 m). Where possible, tolerate a certain amount of growth, since the tiny flowers nourish pollinators including butterflies. It can also be used as a sharp-flavored salad before it flowers.

Hairy bittercress is common in garden centers and nurseries, so it is easily imported to gardens. The eventual size depends on growing conditions. In dry conditions even very small plants can set seed that persists in the soil, and as this weed's life cycle can be as little as 12 weeks it can become very numerous. Wavy bittercress (*Cardamine flexuosa*) and New Zealand bittercress (*Cardamine corymbosa*) are also common in nurseries, and may occur with retail plants, and are dealt with as for hairy bittercress.

Management
Hoeing is effective, but because stem sections can re-root, remove and destroy severed plants. Hand-weeding is easy, and mulching will prevent emergence. Remove and bury the top level of potting mix in newly bought plants to avoid new growth.

BITTERCRESS

ABOVE Oval cotyledons
are followed by long-stalked,
kidney-shaped, hairy
first leaves.

ABOVE RIGHT Long
stalks carry lobed leaflets
in opposite pairs and tiny,
white, four-petaled flowers.

RIGHT The small rosettes of
this weed can be easily lifted
with a hoe or by hand.

WHITE

Chenopodium album

Fat hen, lamb's quarters

Height 8 in–6½ ft (20 cm–2 m)

Spread 8–12 in (20–30 cm)

Seeds Mid- to late summer, fall, up to 20,000 per plant

Germinates Spring, summer, and early fall

Where it grows Very common on cultivated ground

A very variable annual plant with massive seed production, white goosefoot is highly efficient at using soil nutrients and water, especially in fertile vegetable gardens, starving as well as overshadowing crops. The gray-green diamond-shaped leaves are followed by inconspicuous wind-pollinated spikes of green flowers. Some seeds germinate immediately after shedding, but most become dormant; they are a valuable source of food for birds.

In many parts of the world, white goosefoot is a valued vegetable, and indeed it was considered such in Britain until the 17th century, when cabbages and spinach supplanted it. Common orache (*Atriplex patula*) is similar but has sharp points at the base of its leaves, is more spreading, and has green undersides to seedling leaves. Control measures are similar.

Management
Prevention of seed set is vital. Seedlings quickly grow into sturdy young plants that readily re-root after hoeing, so collection or hand-weeding is essential, and easily done. Ideally, cut large weeds into a bucket to prevent seed shed and destroy them, then dig out the roots. Mulches before weed emergence are also effective.

GOOSEFOOT

TOP The elongated seedling leaves often have bright purple undersides and are carried on a purplish stem.

ABOVE The tiny green flowers are carried on spikes that originate from the junction of the leaves and stems.

LEFT The leaves are short-stalked and fleshy, usually with toothed edges and a whitish coating on the underside.

HORSEWEED

Conyza canadensis

Canadian fleabane, mare's tail

Height Up to 6 ft (1.8 m)

Spread 8 in (20 cm)

Seeds Summer but mostly fall, 45 per capsule, up to 50,000 per plant

Germinates Fall

Where it grows Cultivated areas, pavements, and open ground

Horseweed is common in human-made environments because it is resistant to glyphosate, the herbicide most used in such places, and its seeds are wind-dispersed. It arrived in the UK 300 years ago, probably from North America, though its real origin is likely to be Asia. The flowers attract insects, including bees and moths, while its seeds support birds, so it has considerable wildlife value.

Although this plant can be taller in fertile soils, it is usually about 2 ft (60 cm) high, with its flowering spike growing from a rosette of leaves, followed by inconspicuous daisylike flowers on numerous branched stalks. There are similar plants—tall fleabane (*Conyza sumatrensis*) and flax-leaf fleabane (*Erigeron bonariensis*)—and these are considered noxious weeds in many places.

Management

Horseweed cannot survive soil disturbance by digging or hoeing. On artificial surfaces, scraping or hot water will destroy young plants. Hand-weeding of the deep-rooted flowering plants is difficult, but it is vital to limit the dispersal of seeds, which can spread on the wind for more than 330 ft (100 m), though they remain only briefly viable in the soil. Mulches are highly effective because the seeds need light to germinate.

TOP Oblong cotyledons are followed by rounded stalked leaves. Forget-me-nots and daisies have similar seedlings.

ABOVE The tiny daisy flowers, tightly enclosed by sepals, have white or pale purple ray petals and a yellow central disk.

RIGHT The flowers are followed by hairy seed heads that are dispersed by the wind.

JIMSON

Datura stramonium

Thorn apple, devil's snare

Height 3 ft (1 m)

Spread 20 in (50 cm)

Seeds Late summer, fall, 1,400 per plant

Germinates Summer

Where it grows
Fertile disturbed ground, open ground

This narcotic and toxic plant gained the name of jimson weed in North America from the intoxication of soldiers at Jamestown, Virginia, who ingested a preparation of it in 1676 and became mildly deranged for around a week. Consumption is hazardous. It is widespread in hot regions and is considered a particular problem in soybean fields because it competes for the same nutrients.

The broad, coarsely toothed leaves and purple, hairless stems carry conspicuous large white or purple trumpet flowers followed by spiny fruits, each containing 600–700 seeds. The plant is rank-smelling. Rough cocklebur (*Xanthium strumarium*), another American native, has similar spiny fruits but lacks the divided leaves and rank odor of jimson weed. It is sometimes found in the UK as a contaminant of bird seed.

Management
Jimson weed relishes high fertility and is particularly vigorous in very fertile soils and around manure and compost piles. Hoeing is fairly effective and mulching can prevent its growth. Because seeds can remain dormant but viable in the soil for up to 40 years, seeding must be prevented by hand-weeding if necessary. Gloves are advisable. Plants must be destroyed or thoroughly composted to ensure seed destruction.

WEED

ABOVE LEFT The leaves are at first an elongated oval shape, becoming irregular with maturity.

ABOVE Maturing plants, bearing conspicuous trumpet flowers, become highly branched, shed lower leaves, and dominate nearby vegetation.

LEFT The flowers are followed by spiky "thorn apple" fruits containing numerous small black seeds.

PETTY

Euphorbia peplus

Milkweed, cancer weed, radium weed

Height 12 in (30 cm)

Spread 4 in (10 cm)

Seeds Summer, fall, 700 per plant

Germinates Spring

Where it grows Any disturbed ground

This little annual is upright, usually single-stemmed, sometimes branched, with pale green leaves. The stems bear distinctive tiny green flowers that lack petals and are surrounded by pale green bracts. Though they are rich in pollen and nectar, petty spurge flowers and seeds freely with or without insect pollination; the seeds germinate within 12 months and only a few persist. Petty spurge is a significant weed in North America and Australia, though it is originally from Asia, Europe, and North Africa.

Like all euphorbias, petty spurge exudes an irritant toxic sap when it is broken, potentially causing irritation to the skin, lips, and eyes. Handle it only when wearing gloves and avoid touching your face before you have washed your hands thoroughly. The sap has medical applications in suppressing skin lesions including certain skin cancers, confirming its folk medicine use in treating warts and blemishes. Sun spurge (*Euphorbia helioscopia*) is similar but less pervasive and has an umbrellalike structure, unlike the upright petty spurge.

Management
Hoeing, mulches, and hand-weeding are highly effective in preventing petty spurge from flowering and producing seeds.

SPURGE

TOP The oval paired cotyledons are hairless and are supported by a short stalk. Although the first true leaves arise in a pair, later leaves form one at a time.

ABOVE Slender and delicate, the plants are topped by their distinctive green bracts.

RIGHT The tiny seeds are scattered as the seed capsules burst. Ants collect and distribute them farther afield.

KEW

Galinsoga parviflora

Gallant soldier

Height 8–20 in (20–50 cm)

Spread 6–12 in (15–30 cm)

Seeds Summer to fall, 2,000 per plant

Germinates Late spring, summer, early fall

Where it grows Moist, fertile, cultivated ground in sun or light shade

A frost-sensitive annual from the daisy family, *Galinsoga parviflora* is probably an escapee from the Royal Botanic Gardens, Kew, where it was introduced from Peru in 1796. It has simple leaves, fleshy stems, and white, yellow-centered flowers. Some flowers have a hairy tuft on the seeds, which helps them spread about 90 ft (30 m) on the wind; the abundant seeds, nectar, and pollen all sustain wildlife.

The seeds lie dormant in the soil for at least two years, germinating when exposed to light and the soil is warm enough. The plants then grow fast, with the potential for several generations before frosts kill them. Shaggy soldier (*G. quadriradiata*) is almost identical, but more hairy.

Management
Prevent seed set by frequent hoeing and hand-weeding before plants flower. Burn uprooted plants or bury them deeply as they can still produce viable seeds. Mulching or dense cover crops will prevent *Galinsoga* growing. Shaggy soldier is similarly managed.

WEED

TOP The first true leaves are four in number, rounded to triangular in shape.

ABOVE Clusters of tiny blooms with white ray flowers surrounding yellow disk flowers are carried on upright, highly branched, hairy shoots.

RIGHT The leaves are egg-shaped to lance-shaped, with toothed edges that have fine hairs.

CLEAVERS

Galium aparine

Sticky willy, goosegrass, catchweed bedstraw

Height Up to 6½ft (2 m)

Spread Up to 6½ft (2 m)

Seeds Late summer, early fall, 350 per plant

Germinates Spring, late summer, early fall, peaking after the first frosts

Where it grows Hedges and on open ground, only problematic on fertile disturbed soil

Cleavers is a scrambling annual that grows swiftly from spring-germinating seeds or overwinters from fall-germinating seeds then surges in spring weather.

The sticky seeds enable it to hitch rides on animals to aid its spread, though they are a torment to pet-owners trying to brush them away. It favors wet weather and highly fertile soil, where the plants rapidly grow into a thick mass of entangled stems that can swiftly overwhelm garden plants. Some drought tolerance is provided by their strong roots. Cleavers support many caterpillars, including those of the hummingbird hawk moth. Speedwells (p.76) have a similar sprawling habit but are much less competitive.

Management
Prevent seed from setting by hoeing at an early stage before cleavers become embedded in garden plants, followed later by hand-pulling or raking. Seeds can persist in the soil for up to five years. Mulches are highly effective.

TOP The oval cotyledons have a distinctive terminal notch. Similar seedlings include ivy-leaved speedwell seedlings with longer leaf stalks, while hemp-nettles (*Galeopsis* spp.) have leaves that are more rounded.

ABOVE Sticky, hairy, square stems and whorls of sticky leaves with tiny white flowers in clusters along the stem are characteristics of cleavers.

RIGHT The flowers quickly give rise to seeds, which need winter chill before they can germinate.

HIMALAYAN

Impatiens glandulifera

Himalaya touch-me-not, ornamental jewelweed

Height 6–10 ft (2–3 m)

Spread 12–16 in (30–40 cm)

Seeds Late summer, 800 per plant

Germinates Spring

Where it grows Damp soil, on the banks of streams and rivers

This Himalayan native is now a global species due to spread by humankind. Introduced as a garden plant to Britain in 1839, it has spread into North America, where it is considered to be highly invasive in several states. It produces high yields of nectar, which is appreciated by beekeepers and supports pollinators, but it also suppresses and destroys native vegetation, particularly on riverbanks, leaving them open to erosion. On balance it has a negative effect on the environment.

The tall, lush plants grow all summer, flowering from June to October with pink-purple, occasionally white, helmet-shaped flowers. The subsequent seed pods burst explosively when ripe, scattering seed for up to 23 ft (7 m). Japanese knotweed (p.114) and giant hogweed (*Heracleum mantegazzianum*) also grow rampantly in moist situations but have quite different flowers and leaves. The latter is potentially harmful and if it is seen, expert help should be sought.

Management
It spreads via seeds, often waterborne by streams, ditches, and floods, but the plant is occasionally (and inadvisedly) sown by gardeners. Seeds can remain viable for two years. Manage by mowing or hand-pulling to prevent seeding. In the long term, biological control by an introduced rust fungus may curb this weed.

BALSAM

ABOVE LEFT Broad, almost square cotyledons are followed by elongated true leaves.

ABOVE Reddish stems carry lance-shaped leaves with serrated edges.

LEFT The attractive seed heads burst when ripe, scattering their seeds.

PRICKLY

Lactuca serriola

Compass plant, milk thistle

Height 3–6 ft (1–2 m)

Spread 16–24 in (40–60 cm)

Seeds Early fall, 15,000 per plant

Germinates Spring, early fall

Where it grows Open ground, roadsides, walls, disturbed soil

This stiff, erect annual plant carries broad, oblong, prickly leaves with pale midribs that diminish in size the higher up on the plant they are. The upper leaves twist following the sun's passage, hence the common name of "compass plant." The often bristly stems are topped by branching sprays of pale yellow flowers. Rich in pollen and nectar, they are relished by pollinators, notably bees. Broken stems exude copious, milky, latex-rich sap.

Native to Europe, Asia, and North Africa, this weed was accidentally introduced to North America in the 1890s. Prickly lettuce was once quite scarce in the UK, mainly found in gravel pits, but extensive 1930s arterial road construction allowed wide distribution in road stone. Later, bombed cities provided an ideal environment. Great lettuce (*Lactuca virosa*) is less prickly and has a maroon stem and midribs. It is found in the same disturbed environments, though is less widespread, and is controlled in the same way.

Management
Prevention of seed formation, by hand-weeding if necessary, is the best control as buried seeds may remain viable for three to six years. Young plants are vulnerable to hoeing and stale seedbeds (p.135) and are prevented by mulch.

LETTUCE

TOP LEFT Round or oval seedlings, notched at the tip, are followed by a rosette of true leaves.

ABOVE Erect pale stems arise from the rosette, supporting leaves that characteristically clasp the stem. Flowers are produced in terminal and side shoots.

TOP RIGHT Flowers bloom over a long period, so flowers and the seeds are commonly present together.

RED

Lamium purpureum

Red archangel

Height 4–16 in (10–40 cm)

Spread 4–12 in (10–30 cm)

Seeds Summer, fall, 1,000 per plant

Germinates Spring, summer, fall

Where it grows Fertile, light, cultivated soils

Red dead-nettles are small, bushy plants with tiny pink-red flowers, particularly valued in spring as a source of nectar and pollen for insects including bees and hoverflies at a time when they build their nests. The tubular flowers are especially important for long-tongued bees, including red mason bees and bumblebees. Moth caterpillars such as the garden tiger moth also feed on the foliage. While red deadnettles are annuals, they may overwinter as a green plant. Henbit dead-nettle (*Lamium amplexicaule*) is very similar when young.

Management
Seeds can persist in the soil for more than five years, requiring light to germinate. Mulches of black sheeting or an organic mulch 3 in (8 cm) deep in early winter prevent early spring problems. Preventing seed set by hoeing and hand-pulling is effective; however, given the value of red dead-nettle to insects, delaying removal until seed set will help wildlife.

DEAD-NETTLE

TOP Rounded, blunt-ended cotyledons are carried on long stalks that connect with the leaf indentations. The first true leaves are oval and hairy, with branched veins and toothed edges.

ABOVE Young plants carry whorls of bright flowers that conspicuously surround upright stems. The heart-shaped, tooth-edged leaves are frequently purple-tinted.

RIGHT The tiny egg-shaped seeds, four per flower, are coated with oil to encourage ants to carry seeds about locally.

FIELD

Myosotis arvensis

Scorpion grass

Height 4–20 in (10–50 cm)

Spread 4–12 in (10–30 cm)

Seeds Summer, 1,500 per plant

Germinates Spring, fall

Where it grows Cultivated and other bare soil

Field forget-me-not is a small, soft, slightly hairy plant arising from a basal rosette, bearing flower stalks with distinctive blue blooms that are highly attractive to pollinators such as bees and butterflies. It is also a food plant for caterpillars. Plants, including seedlings, can overwinter to flower the following summer, but it can also behave as an annual. Seeds persist in the soil for several years, but are not notably long-lived.

The common winter bedding forget-me-not has somewhat weedy properties, readily self-seeding, but is very susceptible to powdery mildew that limits its growth. In gardens it can be hard to distinguish the two forget-me-nots. The seedlings resemble those of English daisies (*Bellis perennis*, p.90) but the daisy cotyledons are hairless.

Management
Stale seedbeds (p.135) and mulches can prevent the growth of field forget-me-not. Hoeing is highly effective but some hand-pulling might be necessary, too. Overwintering plants can be suppressed by a thick cover crop or a mulch of rotted compost or other organic matter.

FORGET-ME-NOT

BELOW LEFT Cotyledons are small, dark green, rounded, and hairy. True leaves, also hairy, open one at a time, rather than in pairs.

LEFT The small, famously blue flowers of forget-me-nots attract valuable pollinators to the garden.

BELOW Forget-me-nots may survive through the winter or behave like an annual.

CREEPING

Oxalis corniculata

Creeping oxalis, yellow sorrel

Height Up to 4 in (10 cm)

Spread 4–20 in (10–50 cm)

Germinates Summer and fall

Seeds Late summer and fall, up to 26,000 per plant

Where it grows Any sunny cultivated ground, containers, lawns, and especially greenhouses

Creeping wood sorrel is an herbaceous perennial that flourishes in both tropical and temperate regions, but its origin is unknown. Considered food in many cultures and also used as an herb, it was probably deliberately introduced into regions where it is now a weed. It is widespread in plant nurseries and moves with container-grown garden plants to new gardens. Garden harm is mostly cosmetic, as it is low-growing and uncompetitive, but it can multiply at speed. However, the yellow flowers provide nectar for bees and butterflies.

The clump-forming, pink-flowered *Oxalis debilis* and *O. latifolia* are similar, but unlike *O. corniculata* they have bulbs that can remain viable for several years. All have cloverlike leaves.

Management
Hoeing, digging out, and hand-weeding to prevent seed set are key. Rake out wood sorrel in a lawn, then boost the grass with lawn fertilizer to smother surviving plants. In severe cases, reseeding after stripping turf is the only solution. Check new plants for signs of wood sorrel and eliminate it before introducing them to your garden.

WOOD SORREL

TOP The oval cotyledons have vertical edge hairs, followed by the heart-shaped first true leaves that arise in threes.

ABOVE Bright green leaves with three leaflets and purple-leaved forms are common, bearing clusters of five-petaled, yellow, self-pollinated flowers in the leaf axils.

RIGHT Although stems root where they touch the ground, seeds, released explosively from the cylindrical seed pods, are the main means of garden spread.

SMARTWEED

Persicaria maculosa

Willow weed, persicary, red leg, lady's thumb, redshank

Height 12–24 in (30–60 cm)

Spread 16–24 in (40–60 cm)

Seeds Summer, fall, 500 per plant

Germinates Spring

Where it grows Disturbed bare soil, usually clay-rich

This sprawling, frost-sensitive annual sends up flowering stems bearing dense spikes of pink flowers that attract butterflies, bees, and hoverflies. The characteristic dark blotch in the center of the leaf has given rise to alternative names such as "lady's thumb," "Virgin Mary's thumb-mark," and less attractively, but perhaps understandably given its pernicious nature, "devil's arsewipe." It is highly competitive with garden plants. Mature plants retain their shiny, hard, brown seeds, which are shed when the plants are disturbed. Dormant when shed, they become viable after about two months, persisting in the soil for more than five years.

Pale smartweed (*Persicaria lapathifolia*) differs in having silvery hairs on its first true leaves, which are long and narrow. This common weed may hybridize with smartweed, producing plants with intermediate characteristics. They are similarly managed.

Management
Prevention of seed production is crucial by mulching to prevent germination, hoeing young plants, and hand-weeding where necessary. Fragments produced by hoeing can re-root at the nodes. Even young plants can flower and set seed, necessitating vigilance. Liming acid soils to raise the pH helps.

TOP The first true smartweed leaves are broad and dark green, often tinged with red. They are carried on hairless plants, following elongated, narrow, stalkless cotyledons with a reddish stem. Seedlings become silvery gray.

RIGHT Later leaves develop a central dark blotch on sprawling plants often with reddish-tinted stems bearing many upright flower shoots.

ABOVE The tiny flowers are held in short, dense spikes, ranging from pale to dark pink, resembling seeds.

ANNUAL

Poa annua

Causeway grass, annual meadow grass

Height 2–12 in (5–30 cm)

Spread 8 in (20 cm) or more

Seeds Spring to fall, 10–500 per plant

Germinates All year round

Where it grows Bare, disturbed soils

Grasses are common weeds, but most are less persistent, fecund, and competitive than annual bluegrass. This plant swiftly colonizes bare patches of fertile soil, forming tufts of bright green leaves on short, weak stems, almost always in flower, with open, pyramidal, green flower heads. It competes poorly with dense plantings, but can be a problem in seedbeds. However, while seeds are easily spread on mowers, boots, and tools, their viability declines rapidly in cultivated soil. Small mammals such as voles graze annual bluegrass, and the seeds are important winter food for birds, especially finches.

The life cycle of annual bluegrass takes as little as six weeks in summer, and because it is tolerant of trampling underfoot it is common in lawns, but browns readily in dry weather and becomes unsightly. It is highly variable in habit, with purple-leaved forms and some perennial populations.

Management
Larger plants re-root after hoeing, but digging and burying is effective. Hand-weeding is laborious but often unavoidable. In lawns, overseeding using lawn seed mixtures suited to soil and site after close mowing with clippings removed can successfully squeeze out annual bluegrass. Mulches can prevent seedlings in beds.

BLUEGRASS

TOP The seedlings are hard to distinguish from those of other grasses.

ABOVE Annual bluegrass is nearly always in flower.

RIGHT Bare patches of soil may be soon colonized with spreading patches of bluegrass.

PROSTRATE

Polygonum aviculare

Iron grass, knotweed

Height 2–24 in (5–60 cm)

Spread 4–39 in (10–100 cm)

Seeds Summer, fall, 1,000 per plant

Germinates Spring, early summer

Where it grows Cultivated or other disturbed soil

Knotweed forms a low, spreading, matted growth of wiry stems and narrow leaves carrying tiny pink-and-white flowers in summer and fall that is very hard to pull up due to the tenacious roots. The seeds are triangular and shed over a long period in summer and fall. It is highly competitive and in thick vegetation can grow upward in smothering masses. However, birds and small mammals often feed on it in high summer, so leave it to grow where possible.

The seeds of knotgrass germinate in spring, becoming dormant when warm summer weather arrives; fall-germinating plants are killed by winter weather. The cotyledons of white goosefoot (*Chenopodium album,* p.34) are similar but mealy.

Management
Mulches are effective, but hoeing must be done early because larger plants can re-root. Hand-weeding is often needed because preventing seed production is essential. The seeds are very long-lived in the soil, germinating only when exposed to light by cultivation, so this plant can also be countered by no-dig methods.

KNOTWEED

TOP Long, narrow cotyledons carried on a crimson stem are upward-pointing at a slight angle to each other rather than opposed. The first true leaves are relatively broad.

RIGHT Tiny white or pink flowers are borne in the leaf axils rather than the stem ends. The nodes of the stem are swollen.

GROUNDSEL

Senecio vulgaris

Chickenweed, birdseed, old-man-in-the-spring

Height 3–15 in (8–40 cm)

Spread 20 in (50 cm)

Seeds All year, mainly spring and summer, 1,500 per plant

Germinates All year, with spring and fall peaks

Where it grows Cultivated soil and other disturbed environments

Very common in cultivated ground or other disturbed environments, including paved or gravel areas, groundsel has several life cycles during the growing season. Groundsel can behave as an ephemeral, annual, overwintering annual, or biennial, perhaps explaining its ubiquity. Its airborne seeds, up to as many as 1,500 per plant, are a good source of food for birds such as finches and sparrows. The plant is also useful for pollinating insects and supports the caterpillars of cinnabar moths.

Groundsel forms a rosette initially before sending up stems with the indented, ragged leaves arranged in a spiral around them. The stems are often very branched and bear tubular yellow flowers, followed by fluffy white seed heads. This plant often grows beneath taller garden plants—even weak plants can set some seed.

Management
Its capacity for spread makes groundsel potentially very competitive for space in the garden. Control it by removing plants before the seeds set. Even young plants will form a few viable seeds if they are left on the soil surface, or even composted, so groundsel plants should be destroyed or buried deeply. Hoeing is highly effective and the plants are also easily pulled up by hand.

ABOVE LEFT Young plants form a rosette of leaves before developing a flowering stem.

ABOVE The small, yellow, tubular flower heads are borne on slender stems.

LEFT Fluffy white seed heads that are easily spread by the wind follow the flowers.

BLACK

Solanum nigrum

Garden nightshade, houndberry

Height 28 in (70 cm)

Spread 24 in (60 cm)

Seeds Summer, early fall, 500 per plant

Germinates Late spring, summer

Where it grows Cultivated ground, open ground, orchards

These bushy, upright plants carry white, tomato-like flowers in clusters of about eight that attract pollinators. They are highly variable and some subtypes have been recognized. Whether black nightshade is poisonous is unclear; edible cultivars have small, tomato-like, musky black fruits that are used for pie fillings, for example, but given the uncertainty, no part of uncultivated black nightshade should ever be consumed. However, birds relish these fruits with no ill effect, distributing seeds in their droppings.

Several similar plants can occur in gardens. Enchanter's nightshade (*Circaea lutetiana*) is not a true nightshade, though woody nightshade (*Solanum dulcamara*) is. Both are perennials that thrive in unkempt garden areas, but are not prolific seed producers. They can be dug out where they are unwanted but both have some value to wildlife.

Management
Black nightshade can carry viruses, including tomato mosaic virus. Hoeing is highly effective, but some plants can be missed in dense planting and should be hand-weeded before seed is set. Buried seeds become dormant and survive for at least five years. Plant or sow heavily infested areas in late spring, which gives an opportunity to use the stale seedbed method (p.135). Mulches prevent seedlings from establishing.

NIGHTSHADE

LEFT The paired, elongated oval cotyledons are hairy and often purplish.

ABOVE LEFT The tomato-like flowers are characteristic of nightshade. The leaves are oval to triangular and have pointed tips.

ABOVE The plant's spherical fruits ripen to glossy black and are popular with birds.

COMMON

Sonchus oleraceus

Milk thistle, hare's thistle, milky tassle

Height 2–3 ft (60–90 cm)

Spread 18-24 in (45–60 cm)

Seeds Late spring, summer, early fall, 20,000 per plant

Germinates Fall, spring, early summer

Where it grows Cultivated ground and open areas

Sowthistle is a branched, upright annual but often overwintering plant with gray-green leaves bearing masses of bright yellow dandelion-like flowers, followed by fluffy wind-borne seeds. This native of Europe and Asia is valuable for wildlife, in particular hoverflies; their larvae are voracious predators of greenfly and other unwelcome insects. However, it does act as host to viruses that can infect garden plants and some damaging greenfly and nematodes in North America, where it is an invasive nonnative weed.

Other sowthistles with weedy behavior include perennial sowthistle (*Sonchus arvensis*), which has tiny glandular hairs on the flowering shoots, and spiny sowthistle (*S. asper*), with rich green, prickly leaves, reddish stems, and rounded bases that grip the stem.

Management
Hoeing, mulches, and hand-weeding prevent seed formation, which is crucial for managing this plant. Seeds can remain viable in the soil for at least five years.

SOWTHISTLE

TOP Young plants have narrow, deeply toothed true leaves following smooth, oval cotyledons. As days shorten in the fall, late-germinating plants form overwintering rosettes.

RIGHT Long, narrow-toothed leaves, ending in a triangular lobe, clasp the hairy stems, which are full of milky sap. Yellow, flask-shaped flowers are carried in open clusters.

ABOVE The seed heads are loose, fluffy, and white, carried up to 23 ft (7 m) in dry weather. Seeds become viable within a week of flowering.

COMMON

Stellaria media

Chicken weed, white bird's ear

Height Prostrate but up to 12 in (30 cm) at flowering

Spread More than 12 in (30 cm)

Seeds Summer and fall, 2,500 seeds per plant

Germinates Fall and winter

Where it grows Fertile cultivated ground

This bright green, white-flowered, matted ground cover plant grows lushly in summer and in winter on uncropped fertile soil that is not acidic. Although it protects bare soil it can smother overwintered vegetables. Chickweed seeds are food for birds such as mourning doves and are also eaten by insects, including some ground beetles. Its young leaves are eaten by birds and make a rather earthy winter salad, too.

An annual plant, chickweed has up to three generations per year, flowering at all seasons and producing seeds that remain viable for more than five years. It can overwhelm seedlings of garden plants, carry viruses, and rapidly build up a large and persistent soil seed bank. Common mouse-ear chickweed (*Cerastium fontanum*) is very similar, and is controlled in the same way.

Management
Preventing seed production and re-rooting of fragments is vital. Digging and hoeing in dry, warm weather kills young weeds but older weeds are too tangled to hoe, although raking can uproot many. Stale seedbeds (p.135) are highly effective. Hand-weeding chickweed in dense plantings is effective if the root is identified and pulled up.

CHICKWEED

TOP Oval, slightly pointed cotyledons are rapidly followed by true leaves in pairs.

RIGHT The true leaves, more than ⅜-in (8-mm) long, are slightly pointed on round stems, with one line of hairs.

ABOVE Chickweed grows in a spreading mat of lush, tangled foliage.

FIELD

Thlaspi arvense

Dish mustard, stinkweed

Height 6–8 in (15–20 cm)

Spread 3–6 in (8–15 cm)

Seeds Summer, fall, 2,000 per plant

Germinates Spring, fall, winter

Where it grows Cultivated or open ground

This is an upright annual plant that bears rounded leaves with a wavy margin, but does not form rosettes. It has a fetid smell when crushed. Pennycress flowers offer valuable nectar and pollen to insects early in the spring; they are followed by rounded, notched fruit capsules thought to resemble pennies, hence the common name. Shepherd's purse (*Capsella bursa-pastoris*, p.30) is similar but arises from rosettes and has heart-shaped seed pods.

As with many plants in the brassica family, pennycress has seeds that are rich in oil, so the potential of this species as a biofuel crop to replace fossil fuels in the struggle against climate change is being explored.

Management
Stale seedbeds (p.135) and mulches prevent this annual weed, which should not be allowed to set seed in the garden. It is highly susceptible to hoeing, but hand-weeding may also be required. While pennycress overwinters readily, thick cover crops can suppress it, as can mulches of well-rotted compost.

PENNYCRESS

TOP Light green, broadly oval cotyledons are carried on long stalks, often with a downturned tip. Rounded true leaves with a slightly wavy edge follow.

ABOVE Upright, hairless stems carry stalked lower leaves. The small white flowers open in spring, providing an early source of food for pollinating insects.

RIGHT The flat, winged, deeply notched fruits contain up to 14 small black seeds, shed over a number of weeks as fruits ripen in succession up the stem.

ANNUAL

Urtica urens

Small nettle

Height 6–24 in (15–60 cm) tall

Spread 10 in (25 cm)

Seeds Late summer, early fall,
100–1,000 per plant

Germinates Spring to fall,
peaking in early summer

Where it grows Cultivated
fertile ground

A sharp stinging sensation on ungloved hands while harvesting vegetables or pulling weeds is often the first unwelcome indication of this compact annual plant. However, birds relish its seeds, it has herbal uses, and it is a rather stringy spinach substitute. Small, green flowers, male and female on the same plant, are borne on branched upright stems clothed with oval, toothed, stalked, dark green leaves, with all parts covered in stinging hairs. Seed is set from June, but the plant continues to grow, flowering and shedding more seeds as it goes. Early seeds can germinate immediately, while later seeds lie dormant until the following year. Seeds remain viable in the soil for more than five years.

The common nettle (*Urtica dioica*), usually found in uncultivated ground, grows much larger (4 ft/1.2 m) and is more important in supporting the caterpillars of red admiral, small tortoiseshell, painted lady, and comma butterflies.

Management
Preventing seeds being set is vital. Hoe seedlings as soon as seen and hand-weed plants before they grow large. Thick crops that shade the weeds greatly reduce seed set, while mulches prevent seeds germinating.

NETTLE

TOP Seedling leaves are oval with a tiny terminal notch. They are followed by deep green, heavily notched, hairy leaves.

ABOVE Clusters of green male and female flowers are carried on the stems of mature plants.

LEFT Seeds retain parts of the flower, enabling them to cling to clothing or fur, enhancing dispersal.

IVY-LEAVED

Veronica hederifolia

Corn speedwell, ivy chickweed, winter-weed

Height 2–6 in (3–15 cm)

Spread Up to 18 in (45 cm)

Seeds Spring, 80 per plant

Germinates Early spring, late fall, winter

Where it grows Hedges, grass, and cultivated ground

Speedwells are cheerful garden plants with neat, small, ivy-shaped foliage and attractive blue flowers. There are very similar species that typically infest or, according to your point of view, beautify lawns—corn speedwell (*Veronica arvensis*), slender speedwell (*V. filiformis*), thyme-leaved speedwell (*V. serpyllifolia*), germander speedwell (*V. chamaedrys*), bird's-eye speedwell (*V. persica*), and green field speedwell (*V. agrestis*).

The equally charming ivy-leaved speedwell favors cultivated ground, where bird's-eye and green field speedwell may also be encountered. It is a creeping, rapidly spreading annual with small, pale lilac flowers and five-pointed leaves, and produces heart-shaped fruits. The whole plant is hairy. Ground ivy (*Glechoma hederacea*) is similar in its habit, flowers, and leaves.

Management
Hoeing young plants, raking up older plants and hand-weeding prevents seed production. Seeds remain viable in the soil for more than five years, but mulches prevent seedlings. In lawns, speedwells are notoriously intransigent and resist herbicides. Feeding lawns to encourage grass and mowing after lifting the plants by raking can help manage unwanted plants.

SPEEDWELL

TOP The cotyledons are large and dull green, resembling those of cleavers (p.44) except that they have no notch and are slightly pointed, with terminal swelling.

RIGHT Tiny pale lilac or blue flowers appear at the top of stems.

ABOVE Densely hairy, the leaves have 3–5 lobes. Seeds are heart-shaped and hairy.

WHAT IS A PERENNIAL WEED?

Plants that persist for more than two seasons are called perennials. Some are herbaceous, dying down in winter, which is a great strategy for a weed as it exactly mimics asparagus, strawberries, and the herbaceous perennial ornamental plants that are especially prized by gardeners. Many of the most feared weeds are herbaceous perennials, including ground elder (p.86), hedge bindweed (p.92), and horsetail (p.100).

Some perennial weeds, for example, couch grass (p.96) and nettle, do not fully die down in winter, advertising their presence with young, green shoots. This does not harm their prospects, as the roots of these weeds are notoriously tricky to remove.

Although some perennial weeds—typically those that live in disturbed environments—produce fair numbers of seeds, for example dandelion (p.120) and dock (p.116), other perennial weeds, such as creeping thistles (p.94), spread their roots at the expense of seeds. Seeds are of less use to weeds living in dense vegetation, such as pastures, where there are few opportunities for seeds to settle, but there is ample scope for roots to spread.

Since garden plants are overwhelmingly perennial, perennial weeds are common in gardens. Their massive root systems, rich in buds that can regenerate, are difficult to completely tease out. Ideally, eliminate weeds before planting perennials; it may be necessary to leave the area fallowed for one full growing season.

Imported top soil, often from building sites, can be a potent source of weed seed, so take care when sourcing this—reputable suppliers will be able to provide certification. Horsetail (p.100) and Japanese knotweed (p.114) are spread this way. Manure can also be rich in weed seeds, especially stinging nettles. Fresh manure should be composted before use where possible, before perennials are planted.

Some perennial weeds do not fully die down in winter, advertising their presence with young, green shoots.

YARROW

Achillea millefolium

Milfoil

Height 12–24 in (30–60 cm)
at flowering

Spread Mat-forming, typically
8–12 in (20–30 cm)

Seeds Summer, fall,
900 per plant

Germinates Spring

Where it grows In lawns
and beds

Yarrow is an herbaceous perennial that forms mats of pungent, delicate, gray-green leaves from spreading rhizomes, followed by small white to pink flowers in flat flower heads in summer and fall. It is widespread in wild gardens and meadows, where it is valued for its wildlife benefit, providing both seeds for birds and abundant nectar and pollen for pollinators. However, because it is highly drought resistant, it can overwhelm lawn grasses in dry, infertile soil.

Achillea is named for Achilles, the hero of the Trojan wars, who is reputed to have used the plant to stanch the bleeding wounds of his troops. Modern science has found evidence of its efficacy in wound healing. Chamomile (*Chamaemelum nobile*) and pineappleweed (*Matricaria discoidea*) are similar weeds with feathery foliage but dissimilar flowers.

Management
Improving lawns by feeding, aerating, watering in dry spells, and raking to lift the foliage before frequent mowing, helps limit yarrow. In some cases, digging it out and reseeding with lawn grass is appropriate, but in most lawns, a low level of yarrow can be tolerated.

TOP Thin, narrow cotyledons are followed by typical feathery foliage. They thrive only in open areas and are initially uncompetitive with grasses.

LEFT Flat, clustered heads of small, white or pink flowers sit on top of hairy stems that bear finely divided green-gray leaves.

ABOVE Seed heads that provide food for birds follow the flowers.

GROUND

Aegopodium podagraria

Bishop weed, goutweed

Height Up to 1 ft (30 cm)

Spread 3–5 ft (1–1.5 m)

Seeds Late summer and early fall, few seeds produced

Germinates Spring

Where it grows With perennials, woody plants, and hedges

Ground elder has a long history as a medicinal herb and edible crop, and the young leaves are still eaten in salads today. It often grows in beds and borders planted with perennials, near hedges, or embedded in paving and walls, occasionally escaping from gardens to grow on roadsides, forests, and riverbanks. In spring, three-lobed leaves sprout from soil level, resembling those of shrubby elders—hence the name, though in fact it is not related—and forming thick masses. Flat heads of white flowers bloom in late spring and summer.

Ground elder mainly spreads by its underground rhizomes rather than seeds; rhizome fragments are often introduced to new sites in contaminated soil and garden waste. Bold gardeners grow an attractive ornamental variegated form, *Aegopodium podagraria* 'Variegatum', which is somewhat less invasive but should be carefully watched nonetheless.

Management
Dig out the ground elder, being careful to remove all rhizomes. Infested garden plants nearby often have to be lifted and freed of rhizomes and replanted in weed-free areas. Ground elder is considered an invasive weed in forests and riversides, so it should be destroyed in the garden, not taken elsewhere. To eliminate a patch of ground elder over the course of a summer, smother it with a mulch of black biodegradable plastic, or thick layers of cardboard topped by 6 in (15 cm) of compost.

ELDER

TOP This young plant has lost its distinctive square-ended cotyledons, but the true leaf and climbing habit is already visible.

ABOVE Ground elder carpets the ground and suppresses other plants by shading.

RIGHT Flat, typical carrot family–type flowers abound in summer, producing only modest seed numbers.

WILD

Allium ursinum

Ramsons

Height 20 in (50 cm)

Spread 4–18 in (10–45 cm)

Seeds Summer, but unusual

Germinates Seed unimportant in spread

Where it grows Gardens, forests

Wild garlic is a much-loved native woodland plant and in many cases it is an asset to the garden. This is a bulbous perennial that forms dense colonies of long, elliptical leaves with three-sided, angular flowering stems carrying white spring flowers. It spreads by means of bulb production, and can be troublesome where it is not wanted, but is often prized for its pungent leaves, used raw or cooked for their garlicky flavor. Another wild allium, the chive-like crow garlic (*Allium vineale*) can also be a garden nuisance, but it, too, is used for its garlic-like properties. Its narrow, rounded leaves arise from a bulb, with conspicuous rounded flower heads formed mainly of little purple bulbils that fall to the ground and can remain dormant in the soil for as long as six years. The foliage has a strong onion smell when rubbed.

The related three-cornered leek (*A. triquetrum*), a Mediterranean plant, is particularly invasive and its cultivation is restricted by law in the UK.

Management
Control is difficult and can take several years because inevitably many bulbs remain after digging out or hoeing. Cultivation in winter will disrupt the bulbs at a vulnerable stage, with survivors being hand-weeded out in spring. In extreme cases removing and replacing the soil one spade depth may be necessary. Dispose of bulbs with care as they readily regenerate.

GARLIC

ABOVE LEFT The long, elliptical leaves of wild garlic are fresh green in color.

ABOVE The flowers appear from buds borne in umbels of 6–20.

LEFT The white flowers are attractive, and the scent of garlic from this plant is strong.

ENGLISH

Bellis perennis

Bachelor's button, days-eye, bairnwort

Height 2–6 in (3–15 cm)

Spread 4 in (10 cm)

Seeds Summer to fall, 1,300 per plant

Germinates Mainly summer, but spring and fall, too

Where it grows Short turf and adjacent borders

Daisies are good for pollinating insects and the seeds are consumed by birds, ants, and other wildlife. Both the flowers and leaves are edible and can be sprinkled on salads. A favorite of children, daisies are often unwelcome in formal lawns or sports turf but are esteemed in roadsides, meadows, pastures, and, in moderation, less formal lawns. The rosettes of small, rounded leaves with slightly toothed edges are supported by long, fibrous roots. Thin and hairy, the flower stalks bear small white flowers with yellow centers in all seasons, but especially in spring and summer.

Daisy seeds can lie dormant for four years before a new plant grows. They also spread by means of short runners (side shoots that produce buds). Ox-eye daisy (*Leucanthemum vulgare*) is found in longer grass and considered a valuable wild flower rather than a weed.

Management
A knife or similar tool to remove the rosettes, followed by backfilling with sifted soil and grass seed, is sufficient in most yards. Selective herbicides are used in the sports turf industry, but a more relaxed attitude to these flowers is recommended in gardens. Close mowing will limit seed shedding. Promoting strong grass growth by good lawn care including fertilizer, scarification, aeration, and overseeding with lawn seed will suppress daisies.

DAISY

ABOVE LEFT The first true leaves rapidly develop into flat rosettes.

LEFT The yellow-centered white flowers are enjoyed in informal spaces.

ABOVE This plant continues to produce a few blooms in mild winters.

HEDGE

Calystegia sepium

Bellbind

Size Climbs up to 8 ft (2.4 m)

Spread Trails for more than 6½ ft (2 m)

Seeds Infrequent, in summer

Germinates Spring and fall

Where it grows Uncultivated ground, hedges, shrubberies, fruit orchards

Bindweed is a spectacularly spreading perennial if unchecked. Seeds, which can remain viable for up to 40 years, are rare, but its persistent, thick white rhizomes, mostly buried up to 12 in (30 cm) deep, are widely pervasive. Its prolific, trumpet-shaped summer flowers have charm and also attract bees, moths, and butterflies, while the foliage is food for convolvulus hawkmoth caterpillars.

Management

Digging out the rhizomes is effective, but plants can regenerate from even small fragments. Alternatively, clear infested areas using black plastic sheet or thick organic mulches over several layers of cardboard for one full summer. Another option is to turn such areas into lawn, where mowing eliminates bindweed in two years. In hedges or shrub plantings, cutting and pulling slowly suppresses it. Borders often have to be left fallow for the summer to clear them, while barriers of strong plastic sheeting buried vertically in the soil prevent spread from nearby bindweed colonies.

Where bindweed is embedded in paving, hedges, or other close planting, spot foliage treatment with systemic weedkiller can be used as a last resort. Annual black bindweed (*Fallopia convolvulus*) is readily hoed out. The perennial field bindweed (*Convolvulus arvensis*) is typically found in long grass or uncropped soil. It is less aggressive than bindweed but similarly managed.

BINDWEED

ABOVE Seedlings have squared leaf ends with a slight indentation.

RIGHT The large white trumpet flowers and rambling stems distinguish bindweed.

CREEPING

Cirsium arvense

Canada thistle, prickly thistle

Height 1–4 ft (30–120 cm)

Spread 3–33 ft (1–10 m)

Seeds Late summer, early fall, 4,500 per plant

Germinates Spring, summer, fall

Where it grows Wild gardens and herbaceous borders

Long, spiny, bright green leaves on tall stems typically occurring in rapidly expanding patches characterize the perennial creeping thistle. The seeds are relished by birds, especially goldfinches and linnets, while the larvae of moths and butterflies feed on the foliage. Its flowers are exceptionally nectar- and pollen-rich; a 2016 study of British urban meadows found that creeping thistle was second only to ragwort (*Senecio jacobaea*) in its value to insects, so if gardeners can find ways to contain a patch of this highly invasive, unpleasantly spiny weed they will be doing wildlife much good.

It is primarily a pasture weed, spreading extensively by aggressive creeping roots, but only 3 percent of its seeds are viable. Although its prickly stems deter herbivores, mower blades keep it out of lawns; in less managed places such as perennial borders it can be hard to control. Spear thistle (*Cirsium vulgare*), a biennial, is similar in size and the young plants, both rosettes, are hard to differentiate. It lacks the aggressive roots and does not form patches.

Management
Creeping thistle cannot easily survive in heavily hoed and cultivated areas such as vegetable gardens, but in perennial plantings it is hard to dislodge. Prevention is ideal, with thickly planted or mulched beds that limit seed germination and establishment.

THISTLE

ABOVE LEFT Smooth second
leaves distinguish creeping
thistle from spear thistle, which
has larger, hairy second leaves.

LEFT Young plants form
rosettes from which spiny
flowering shoots arise,
bearing pink-purple flowers.

ABOVE Pale, downy
seed heads persist on dead
stems, but the basal rosette
dies back in winter.

COUCH

Elymus repens

Couch grass, twitch, scutch, quackgrass

Height Up to 2¼ft (70 cm)

Spread 1¾–3 ft (0.5–1m)

Seeds Late summer to early fall, 300 per plant

Germinates Fall

Where it grows With soft fruit plants, in herbaceous borders, and at the bottom of hedges

Couch grass is an important source of food for butterfly and moth caterpillars, which use it for their larvae, so tolerate it where possible. The raw roots are edible when dried and ground, and the leaves and roots can be used as an herbal medicine.

Couch grass is very common in gardens and open ground. Mowing often suppresses it in lawns, but it can dominate unmowed grassland. It rarely flourishes in vegetable gardens, because it is dug out during cultivation. Couch grass spreads using rhizomes and seeds, and produces 30 seeds per flower stem, only half of which are viable. Creeping bentgrass (*Agrostis stolonifera*) is a similar plant with stolons that creep over the surface, rooting at intervals.

Management

The best way to prevent couch grass from taking hold is to ensure that ground is weed-free before planting, then mulch only with rotted materials—avoid fresh manure derived from straw and hay, because couch grass seeds can lie dormant for up to five years. Clear the ground by covering for several summer months with either black plastic sheet or, more sustainably, several layers of cardboard topped with at least 6 in (15 cm) of composted organic matter. In the latter case the compost can be planted and crops grown while the couch grass is being smothered.

GRASS

TOP The rhizomes tend to grow in straight lines, so new, upright shoots appear in rows.

ABOVE Severed rhizomes can quickly develop into new plants.

RIGHT The spikelets (flower buds) lie flat on the tall stems, so the flower heads feel smooth.

WILLOWHERBS

Epilobium species

Fireweed

Size 1–4 ft (30–120 cm)

Spread 8–16 in (20–40 cm)

Seeds Summer to early fall, 400 per capsule, up to 80,000 per plant

Germinates Fall to spring, mainly fall

Where it grows Common on disturbed soil or in gaps in hard surfaces

Rosebay willowherb (*E. angustifolium*), a common perennial native plant, is the most striking epilobium in North America, but there are others, including highly variable hybrids with the fringed willowherb (*E. ciliatum*). Pollinators relish willowherb flowers, while many other insects including hawkmoth caterpillars feed on the foliage.

Mostly small to medium in size, these plants grow as spreading rosettes from overwhelmingly numerous seedlings. The rosettes retrench before flowering in summer, but this is followed by resurgence and further spread. Seeds have only short persistence in the soil. Horseweed (p.36) is a similar plant.

Management
This weed resists herbicides and is common in nurseries, spreading to gardens via seed contamination of purchased plants or by wind-borne seed. Hoeing and hand-weeding, ideally before seed heads form, is very effective. Plants can develop from the roots of older plants, so these must be collected and destroyed. Use very hot water to kill those in paving. Over winter, cover crops and mulches prevent willowherb emergence.

TOP The long, pointed, glossy leaves grow into spreading rosettes with underground stems.

RIGHT Pinkish-purple flowers are borne from mid-spring to early fall.

ABOVE The pale pink flowers develop into fluffy seed heads, with seeds dispersed long distances by the breeze.

HORSETAIL

Equisetum arvense

Mare's tail, field horsetail

Height 10–24 in (25–60 cm)

Spread Up to 12,000 sq yd (10,000 sq m)

Seeds N/A

Germinates N/A

Where it grows Meadows, roadsides, open ground, gardens

Horsetail is more closely related to ferns than flowering plants and dates from the Carboniferous period (325 million years ago). The plants absorb silicon, which is deposited in the stem, making them abrasive and reportedly used as pot scourers in earlier times. The fertile shoots that arise in the spring are short-lived, with a terminal conical cone that emits spores. Subsequent sterile shoots resemble miniature conifers and are gritty when rubbed.

Below ground, an extensive, deeply buried system of black rhizomes and tubers spreads slowly at about 8 in (20 cm) per year. The spores need moisture to germinate, but the mature plants are less dependent on damp soils. Similar plants include true mare's tail (*Hippuris vulgaris*) and *Equisetum hyemale*. Both are aquatic plants, neither of them weeds.

Management
The deeply embedded rhizomes and tubers are almost impossible to eradicate in permanent plantings. However, horsetail is intolerant of cultivation and readily suppressed by digging and hoeing, although it is seldom absolutely eradicated. Shading by trees and shrubs suppresses it, and it cannot survive beneath mowed lawns. Spread via contaminated soil is common, and only soil known to be free of horsetail should be brought into gardens; choose reputable suppliers and check with them.

ABOVE LEFT In spring, fertile stems bear a terminal cone-shaped spore-producing structure.

ABOVE Sterile green shoots develop in summer, bearing bristlelike leaves that nourish the rhizomes.

LEFT Horsetail proliferates in dense masses of foliage that overwhelm other plants.

LESSER

Ficaria verna* subsp. *verna

Pilewort

Height 2–4 in (5–10 cm)

Spread 6 in (15 cm)

Seeds Early summer, 70 per plant

Germinates Spring

Where it grows Woods, hedges, streamsides, and gardens

Lesser celandine is easily recognized by its glossy, green, heart-shaped leaves and the yellow flowers in late winter and spring that offer valuable early nectar and pollen for bees. It dies back underground in summer and needs to experience winter cold before it is able to resprout and flower in spring. Some people may wonder why this pretty, much-loved, herbaceous perennial is treated as a weed, and indeed it can be enjoyed in many situations, as it dies back underground after its brief flowering period. However, it can be unwelcome in lawns and bulb borders. The aquatic marsh marigold (*Caltha palustris*) is similar in that it also flowers early and has glossy leaves but is much larger.

Management
This plant spreads mostly by bulbils (small tubers), which are easily detached during cultivation or weeding. Digging them all out, ideally before flowering, will take several years to achieve eradication. Using spring mulches at least 4 in (10 cm) deep, ideally over a layer of cardboard or black plastic material, may smother celandines. Improving grass swards by feeding and overseeding can make them inhospitable for celandines, causing the plant to decline.

CELANDINE

TOP In late winter or early spring, lesser celandine develops cushions of glossy, green, heart-shaped leaves studded with numerous glossy yellow flowers with 8–12 petals.

ABOVE The tubers are not only part of the root system but are also borne on aerial stems in leaf axils. Their formidable numbers make clearance slow and laborious.

RIGHT The starry yellow flowers are a valuable early source of nectar and pollen for insects

BROADLEAF

Plantago major

Greater plantain, way bread, ribgrass

Size 4–12 in (10–30 cm)

Spread 4–12 in (10–30 cm)

Seeds Summer to fall, 14,000 per plant

Germinates All year round, but mainly mid-spring and late summer

Where it grows Disturbed ground, lawns

Broadleaf plantain is an evergreen perennial that sometimes behaves as an annual with a six-week life cycle. It thrives in compacted soils and closely mowed lawns and is used for repairing damaged ground, where its powerful roots break up hard soils and can also remove harmful chemicals. Although it is potentially wind pollinated, self-pollination is important.

Plantain has great wildlife value as a food plant for insects including caterpillars and moths, and the seed heads persist over winter, providing food for birds; the seeds can remain viable in the soil for more than 20 years. Several other plantains are found in North America, the majority of which were introduced by European settlers.

Management
Plantains can be a benefit where other plants won't grow, but are unwanted in formal lawns. Although they are susceptible to selective weedkillers, good lawn care, especially aeration but also feeding and overseeding bare patches, deters them; deal with any that remain by hoeing all the rootstock.

PLANTAIN

TOP Oblong, hairless cotyledons about ¼-in (5-mm) long on short stalks are followed by oval true leaves. They resemble groundsel (p.64) and dock seedlings (p.116).

ABOVE The myriad minute seeds are often not released from the flower spike until the following year.

RIGHT Greater plantain produces yellowish flowers on short stems from a rosette of broad, oval, prominently-veined leaves. Plants can be tiny in inhospitable places or large in moist, fertile sites.

BRACKEN

Pteridium aquilinum

Brake fern, eagle fern

Height Up to 5ft (1.5m)

Spread Can be more than
6½ft (2m) per year

Seeds Spores are produced
intermittently, perhaps once
a decade

Germinates All year in cool,
moist spots, but spores are
not significant in gardens

Where it grows Spreads in
poor soil and springs back
quickly after fires or logging

Bracken is a tall perennial fern that unfurls from ground level in
spring, developing triangular fronds in three sections that are
bright green in summer, turning red-brown as it dies back
underground in the fall. Its thick, fleshy underground stems
survive winter and potentially spread several yards in summer.
It is widespread in the countryside, where it has some wildlife
value, providing shelter and often nesting sites for mammals,
reptiles, amphibians, birds, and insects; moth caterpillars
feed on it.

In gardens it usually invades from nearby neglected land such
as wooded areas, or arrives in new plants or composted material.
Because it is highly invasive and hard to control, it is unwise to
tolerate bracken in gardens. When plants are mature they shed
spores that are carcinogenic and handling them at this stage is
best avoided.

Management

Persistent cutting or, better, hand-pulling (wearing gloves) will
weaken and gradually eliminate bracken over several years. In
bare ground where other plants are absent it can be dug out.
Systemic weedkillers should be directly targeted without garden
plant foliage being inadvertently treated. However, bracken
does have the advantage that it makes excellent compost.

ABOVE Young fronds unfurl from the base and are very vulnerable to disturbance at this stage, such as repeated trampling.

RIGHT The tall fronds are unmistakable, and ideally pulled while young and consigned to the compost pile where they make good compost.

CREEPING

Ranunculus repens

Creeping crowfoot

Height 6–20 in (15–50 cm) tall

Spread 8–16 in (20–40 cm)

Seeds Summer, fall, 600 per plant

Germinates Spring, summer

Where it grows In moist fertile turf or cultivated soil

An herbaceous perennial with bright yellow flowers and deep green leaves divided into three deeply lobed leaflets, creeping buttercup, along with other buttercups, is widespread in meadows. It has great value for wildlife, with nectar- and pollen-rich flowers, and supports a wide range of insects such as beetles and leafhoppers that feed spiders and birds. In gardens it colonizes lawns and cultivated ground, forming dense clumps with strong, deep roots that embed themselves between garden plants. It spreads by stolons (runners), especially in wet weather, and by seeds that can last more than four years in the soil.

Showy, robust plants, creeping buttercups are often used in wildlife containers that allow biodiversity to be supported even in the smallest spaces. Creeping cinquefoil (*Potentilla reptans*) has a similar spreading habit by stolons, but the leaves are segmented in fives rather than threes. That plant is best managed in a similar way.

Management
In lawns, liming and adding fertilizer to promote grass growth will squeeze it out. In beds and borders, creeping buttercup spreads widely in wet springs. Improving drainage can help limit spread. Digging out or repeated hoeing can also be effective.

BUTTERCUP

ABOVE LEFT Oval
cotyledons are followed
by deeply cut leaves with
three lobes.

ABOVE The familiar yellow
flowers offer plenty of pollen
and nectar for wildlife.

LEFT Creeping buttercup
is well suited to spaces
where wildlife is encouraged
to thrive.

JAPANESE

Reynoutria japonica

Elephant ears, Japanese bamboo, Mexican bamboo, fleece flower

Height 7 ft (2.1 m)

Spread 33 ft+ (10 m+)

Seeds N/A

Germinates N/A

Where it grows Gardens, watersides, and open areas

Japanese knotweed is shy and retiring in its native Japan, where its natural enemies curb its zeal. Where these natural enemies are absent, as in Europe and North America, it has remarkably resilient, deeply creeping roots that are highly resistant to control. Gardeners should seek expert guidance because Japanese knotweed is considered an invasive noxious weed in most if not all states.

It is a handsome plant, introduced as a garden ornamental, that dies back each winter. The following spring it forms reddish, vigorous, hollow shoots carrying spade-shaped green leaves arranged zigzag fashion. The flowers bloom in late summer into the fall, after which dry canes remain when it dies back for the winter. Himalayan honeysuckle (*Leycesteria formosa*), *Houttuynia cordata*, Russian vine (*Fallopia baldschuanica*), and various species of *Persicaria* and *Polygonatum* can appear similar in foliage and habit, but are no cause for concern.

Management

Japanese knotweed is extraordinarily resistant to control. It can be dug out and the root stocks burned or buried very deeply, but any remaining fragment will regrow, so an eradication campaign lasts several years. Powerful weedkillers knock it back but destruction is only certain if no regrowth occurs in the two years post-treatment. To avoid importing it to your garden, introduce only soil that is certified free of perennial weeds.

KNOTWEED

ABOVE LEFT The rhizomes are distinctively massive and woody, supporting vigorous reddish shoots in spring.

ABOVE The flat base of the leaves and tall hollow "canes" are characteristic.

LEFT The zigzag stems and 6-in (15-cm) creamy flower tassels in late summer also identify the plant.

BROAD-LEAVED

Rumex obtusifolius

Bitter dock, bluntleaf dock, dock leaf, butter dock

Height 2–3 ft (60–90 cm) at flowering

Spread 16–24 in (40–60 cm)

Seeds Summer, fall, and early winter, 7,000 per plant

Germinates All year, but peaks in spring and early fall

Where it grows Any fertile cultivated soil or grassland

Broad-leaved dock is an upright perennial arising from a rosette of broad, deep green leaves that dies down in winter. It has a long tap root, branched stems, and sturdy broad leaves. The tough flower spike may be branched with massed clusters of brown flowers. "Dock" derives from the Old English *docce,* meaning "coarse vegetation." It is famously employed to relieve nettle stings, while its use in herbal medicine and salads and for dyeing has also been recorded. Docks support a wide range of insects including leaf beetles, weevils, and capsid bugs, while birds relish the seeds.

Broad-leaved dock is highly variable and also hybridizes with the similar and similarly weedy curled dock (*Rumex crispus*), which favors wetter soils and has narrow, lance-shaped, wavy leaves; reddened stems; and red-green flowers.

Management
The abundant seeds last more than five years in the soil, so preventing seed set is essential. Young plants are easily hoed but older plants can regenerate from upper portions, so it is best to dig out at least the upper half, ideally in spring when the roots are least tenacious. Seeds are often reintroduced via manure from animals fed on contaminated forage. Dock is sensitive to hormone weedkillers.

DOCK

ABOVE LEFT The first true leaves are rounded and broad but indented at the base.

ABOVE Smooth, oblong dock leaves first appear in spring.

LEFT The flowering stems are branched, with clusters of small reddish-brown flowers.

PEARLWORT

Sagina procumbens

Procumbent pearlwort, birdeye pearlwort, matted pearlwort

Height 2 in (5 cm)

Spread Mat-forming

Seeds Summer to fall, 70 per capsule

Germinates All year round

Where it grows Areas with compacted and poorly drained soil

Pearlwort is a tiny evergreen perennial with slender leaves that is sometimes mistaken for moss, though the latter has no roots, nor does it flower. In gardens, pearlwort colonizes paths, lawns, containers, and poorly drained soil where other vegetation does not thrive. These properties, and particularly its resistance to treading, are causing gardeners to seek low-maintenance lawn substitutes that need little fertilizer and water to experiment with pearlwort.

Management
Pearlwort cannot thrive in cultivated areas but does well in compacted soil and open vegetation. In containers, it is associated with over-watering. Hand-weeding is the only remedy in containers and borders. In lawns, good cultivation including scarifying, aerating, feeding, and overseeding bare patches can squeeze pearlwort out. It spreads by fragments or by seeds; ideally, mow infested areas last and then clean the mower. Wax on the leaves largely protects pearlwort from weedkillers.

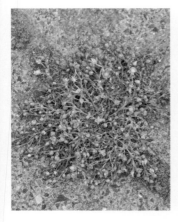

ABOVE Sprawling stems radiate from the initial rosette, eventually forming a mat of narrow leaves often whorled around the stem, terminating in a bristly point. The stems can root as they go.

RIGHT Flowers with tiny white petals, which are often absent, form near the end of the shoots. They are followed by seed pods, initially green, and later white, releasing seeds to be distributed by the wind.

DANDELION

Taraxacum species

One-o-clocks

Height At flowering, 6–12 in (15–30 cm)

Spread 6–10 in (15–25 cm)

Seeds Mainly early to midsummer, 180 per head

Germinates Mainly mid-spring, but sporadic subsequent germination until winter

Where it grows Crops, borders, lawns, perennial garden beds, and long-term containers, especially in alkaline soil

There are more than 200 barely differentiable microspecies of *Taraxacum*, all flowering in summer and often again in the fall. The lance-shaped, deeply lobed leaves form flat rosettes that resist mowing and persist all year. Each plant bears several flowers, the well-known "clocks" producing about 5,000 airborne seeds, with a three-month half-life. Plants can live for more than 10 years.

Dandelion flowers are very valuable to pollinators, while children appreciate the "dandelion clock" seed heads. Each bright yellow flower head is self-fertile and comprises many tiny flowers typical of the Asteraceae (daisy) family. Other rosette-forming lawn weeds include catsear (*Hypochaeris radicata*) and hawkbit (*Leontodon* species), which are also valuable for wildlife.

Management
Ideally, if your neighborhood allows, you can tolerate dandelions for their wildlife benefit. If they multiply too much, digging or lifting with a fork is effective as long as the entire root is removed, since the plant will readily regenerate from root fragments. Hoeing merely distributes root fragments, generating new plants. Mulches prevent seedlings. Cutting before seeds are shed helps, but seeds will drift into the garden from up to 1,640 ft (500 m) away. Lawn weedkillers are a last resort.

TOP Seedlings with elongated, oval, hairless seed leaves are often found in summer and fall.

ABOVE Dandelions flower most profusely in early summer but can still be in bloom in the fall.

RIGHT The familiar dandelion "clocks" are popular with children but release thousands of seeds into the air.

wo

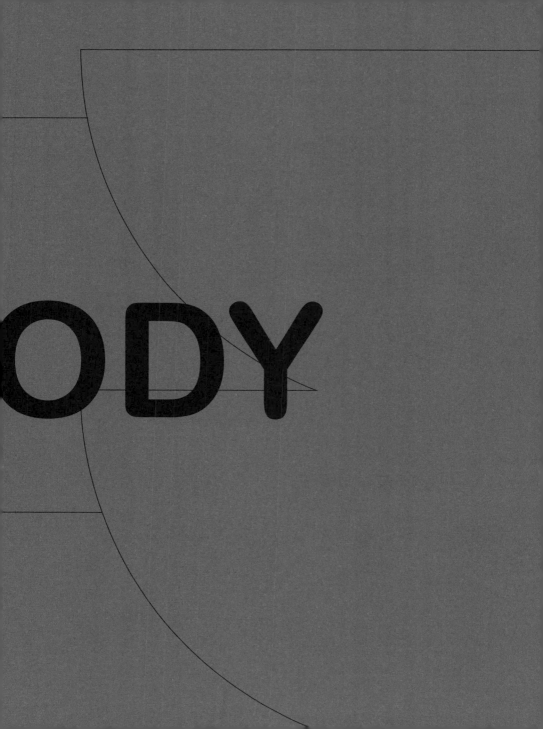

WHAT IS A WOODY WEED?

"Woody" weeds are also perennials (p.80), with their tough stems and shoots remaining all winter. Wild blackberry (p.130) and tree seedlings, such as sycamore maple (p.128), are usually found among other woody plants, such as shrub borders and hedges, where they can be hard to dislodge. Trees produce thousands of seeds, which are dispersed by birds and animals (oaks, hazel, beech) or drift in the air (sycamore, ash, willow).

Unwanted trees and shrubs are easy to see when they are young, especially in winter when other plants die back. They can be cut back or dug out. However, cutting back woody plants induces regrowth, especially if they are cut back in winter, because the plant's resources are in its roots, ready to help the plant rebound in spring. Thickets and sizable saplings form quickly in subsequent years.

Digging out is feasible while a plant is young, but the most persistent woody weeds, including sycamore maple and wild blackberry, have deeply embedded rootstocks. Those become increasingly embedded with time, so dealing with them early is vital because the aerial parts of the plant enlarge until it is a major undertaking to remove them, requiring professional help.

Being taller than most other vegetation, woody weeds are highly competitive, shading out other plants. In gardens without regular maintenance or in semi-wild areas they can develop quickly, growing up to 2 ft (60 cm) per year. Species such as hazel, holly, silver birch, willows, and trees including robinia, Turkey oak, and tree of heaven are common woody weeds. Their spread may be from drifting seeds (birch, willow), birds (hawthorn, wild blackberry, yew) or jays and squirrels (hazel, oaks).

Some welcome these plants as low-cost, wildlife-friendly trees. They can become too large for most yards, but some self-seeding trees, including beech, hazel, hawthorn, oak, and yew, can be dug out as seedlings to make effective and economical hedging plants that are the most wildlife-friendly form of boundary.

"Woody" weeds are usually found among other woody plants, such as shrub borders and hedges.

SYCAMORE

Acer pseudoplatanus

Height More than 40 ft (12 m)

Spread More than 26 ft (8 m)

Seeds Fall

Germinates Spring

Where it grows Forests, open areas, along roadsides

Sycamore maples, being large, produce masses of seeds, which are launched from a lofty position in the tree canopy. The winged seeds can flutter considerable distances in the breeze. Sycamore maple, one of the most common trees, grows vigorously, forming a sturdy sapling in its first year and soon becoming an overbearing small deciduous tree. It can be a handsome spreading tree, but in urban environments it is more often crowded and narrow, disfigured by attempts to control it by pruning.

It has five-lobed deciduous leaves, 4–8 in (10–20 cm) long, and mature trees bear yellow, wind-pollinated spring flowers followed by masses of winged fruit in early fall. Both the seeds and the large number of summer aphids that live on sycamore maples provide food for wildlife such as birds and ladybugs. Sycamore maple seeds, leaves, and seedlings are toxic to horses and great care must be taken to remove seedlings from pastures.

Management
Seedlings in cultivated ground are easily controlled by hoeing but may not be noticed in shrubs and hedges until they become woody plants, at which time they will need to be dug out. If they are just cut back they will regrow from the base. Repeated cutting back will gradually eliminate them where they are too entrenched or inaccessible to be dug out, which can take several years. If this is not possible, the cut surface can be painted with a selective weedkiller.

MAPLE

TOP Seedlings are large, with long cotyledons, quickly followed by heart-shaped true leaves that rapidly develop into the characteristic lobed leaves.

ABOVE The tall, smooth, single stem quickly overtops surrounding vegetation, by which time it has a substantial and stubborn root system. Branching soon follows.

RIGHT The winged seedpods rotate as they fall, which helps them spread farther from the parent tree.

WILD

Rubus fruticosus agg.

Black heg, bramble

Height 5–6½ ft (1.5–2 m)

Spread 6½–10 ft (2–3 m)

Seeds Late summer

Germinates Spring, summer

Where it grows Uncultivated and unmowed areas including hedges, with soft fruit, in asparagus beds, and beneath trees and shrubs

Blackberry biology is complex, with many subspecies and hybrids grouped as "species aggregates." However, the wild blackberry, a deciduous woody perennial, is well known and the fruits are a popular fall treat for jam, jelly, pies, crumbles, and even wine. The flowers are a valuable resource for bees and other pollinators, while birds and mammals spread the seeds via their droppings.

The long, arching, deeply thorny stems of blackberry root as they go, with each tip forming a new plant that can develop into extensive thickets. The deciduous leaves, dark green above and pale beneath, are divided into three or five sections, and are eaten by many native insects. Dewberry (*Rubus caesius*) and feral cultivated blackberries, raspberries, and their hybrids are similar and common, although seldom as troublesome as wild blackberry.

Management
Ideally, dig out wild blackberry bushes while they are still young, because the woody stumps are laborious to remove later. Once they are embedded in hedges or other plantings, control is limited to hard, repeated pruning that may wear the plants down in time. Spot treatment with weedkiller is possible as a last resort, though several applications are typically needed. In grassy areas regular trimming and mowing will gradually eliminate wild blackberries.

BLACKBERRY

ABOVE LEFT The small flowers appear in late spring and may be white or pink.

ABOVE Green at first, the berries ripen to black and are popular with wildlife and gardeners alike.

LEFT The compound leaves have three or five coarsely-toothed, oval leaflets.

GLOSSARY

Acid Of soil, less than pH7, but below pH5.5 if ericaceous ("lime-hating") plants are to thrive.

Alkaline Of soil, greater than pH7, typical of chalky or limestone soils.

Annual A plant that germinates, flowers, and sets seed in one growing season.

Axil The upper angle between a side shoot of a branch and the stem or trunk from which it arises.

Biennial A plant that flowers and sets seed in a second growing season following germination.

Biodiversity net positive An overall beneficial outcome for animals, plants, fungi, and microorganisms that make up the natural world.

Bud bank A weed bud bank is the total viable underground weed buds on roots or rhizomes from which new weeds can arise. See also *seed bank*.

Bulb An underground modified stem that acts as a storage organ while plants are dormant.

Bulbil A small bulb or bulblike growth forming in a leaf axil.

Calyx The collective term for the sepals that form the outer part of the floral envelope.

Contact weedkiller An herbicide that acts by contact, with no movement within the plant. Acetic and pelargonic acids are contact weedkillers.

Cotyledon A primary leaf that either stores food within a seed or grows, becomes green, and photosynthesizes, making food for the seedling.

Cover crops (green manures) Fast-growing plants that cover bare soil, retain nutrients, suppress weeds, and improve soil fertility when incorporated into the soil.

Cross-pollination Transfer of pollen between separate plants, implying cross-fertilization.

Cultivation The act of gardening.

Dormancy Of seeds which cease activity for prolonged periods, until certain conditions, typically temperature and light, are met.

Ephemeral Plant that can germinate, flower, and set seed more than once in a single growing season.

Ericaceous "Lime hating" plants due to their inability to acquire iron from any but acid soils.

Explosive seed pod Seed pod that develops structural tension as it ripens, eventually opening vigorously and hurling weed seeds many yards.

Fallow Ground left bare to give an opportunity to kill weeds.

Fertile Of seeds, capable of germinating; of soil, well provided with plant nutrients and moisture.

Hand-weeding Pulling up weeds by hand, ideally gloved.

Herbicide A pesticide that kills plants.

Hoeing Destroying weeds with a blade that acts on the soil.

Lawn Area of mowed, low-growing vegetation, typically grass, with other plants that survive mowing. Non-grass lawns are a form of perennial border with different weed populations.

Mulch Soil covering that excludes light, killing existing weeds and preventing germination. It may be organic, bark for example, or sheets of black plastic.

Node Joint on stems where leaves, shoots, or flowers are attached.

No-dig Gardening without digging, where weeds have to be managed by mulching, hoeing, or hand-weeding.

Perennial A plant that persists for more than two seasons.

Rhizome A specialized underground or surface stem producing roots, stems, leaves, and flowers along its length.

Runner A common name for a *stolon*.

Seed Ripened, fertile ovule that is an embryonic plant.

Seed bank The weed seed bank is the total viable weed seeds present in the top 10 in (25 cm) or so of soil, derived from newly shed seeds and older dormant ones from previous years.

Selective weedkillers Herbicide that kills some plants without significantly affecting others. Lawn weedkillers are a common example.

Self-fertile Fertilization with pollen from the same plant.

Sepal Part of the flower envelope protecting the inner flower parts. See also *calyx*.

Soilborne Seeds or more commonly root fragments spread by soil movement or transfer.

Spore In effect the "seed" of fungi, ferns, mosses, and horsetail.

Stale seedbed Prepared ground left unsowed to allow weed seeds to germinate. The seedling weeds are destroyed without disturbing the soil, by shallow hoeing, for example. Subsequent sowings have the benefit of reduced weed competition, and therefore less hoeing and weeding.

Stolon An above-ground stem, either creeping or aerial, that gives rise to new plants at its tip or at nodes along its length. Also known as a *runner*.

Systemic weedkiller Weedkillers that move through the plant.

True leaf The first leaves to appear after the cotyledons following germination.

Turf Lawn or other managed grass.

Waterborne Spread by water, typically riverside plants.

Wind-borne Spread by wind, typically by downy or "winged" seeds.

RESOURCES

Books

RHS Weeds: The Beauty and Uses of 50 Vagabond Plants, Gareth Richards, Welbeck, 2021.
Discusses 50 wild plant species, illustrated with botanical images.

Weeds: In Defense of Nature's Most Unloved Plants, Richard Mabey, Ecco Press, 2012.
An artistic and entertaining meditation on rethinking our opposition to weeds.

Weeds of the Northeast, Joseph C. Neal et al, Comstock Publishing Associates, 2023.

The Organic Lawn Care Manual, Paul Tukey, Storey Publishing, 2007.

Websites

USDA Federal Noxious Weed List aphis.usda.gov/plant_ health/plant_pest_info/ weeds/downloads/weedlist. pdf
A reference for which weeds are considered highly invasive and are regulated at the federal level.

Cornell College of Agriculture and Life Sciences: Weed Science cals.cornell.edu/weed-science/weed-identification
Identify your weeds by a process of narrowing by characteristics.

Better Homes & Gardens: 33 Lawn and Garden Weeds: How to Identify and Control Them bhg.com/gardening/pests/ insects-diseases-weeds/ types-of-weeds/
A visual guide to some of the most common weeds in the US and how to get rid of them.

Weed Wrangle weedwrangle.org
A national organization that sponsors one-day area-wide volunteer efforts to remove especially harmful nonnative and invasive plants from public areas and teach people to maintain the areas and add native plants.

Identification apps

ID Weeds, University of Minnesota Extension

Seek

PictureThis Plant Identifier

INDEX

Page numbers in italic refer to the illustrations

A

Acer pseudoplatanus 128, 129
Achillea millefolium 82, *83–5*
acid soils 134
Aegopodium podagraria 86, *87*
   A.p. 'Variegatum' 86
agricultural crops 13
Agrostis stolonifera 96
alkaline soils 134
Alliaria petiolata 22, 23
Allium triquetrum 88
   A. ursinum 88, *89*
   A. vineale 88
Alopecurus myosuroides 13
Ambrosia artemisiifolia 26, *27*
   A. psilostachya 26
Anagallis arvensis 28, 29
annual weeds 8, 18–77, 134
   benefits for wildlife 16
   management 14
   seeds 10
archangel, red 50, 51
Artemisia vulgaris 26
Atriplex patula 34
axillary bud nodes 9
axils 134

B

bachelor's button 90, *91*
bairnwort 90, *91*
balsam, Himalayan 12, 46, *47*

bellbind 92, 93
Bellis perennis 52, 90, *91*
bentgrass, creeping 96
biennials 134
bindweed
   annual black 92
   hedge 13, 80, 92, *93*
biodiversity 6, 7, 16, 134
bird food, spreading weeds 12
birds, benefits of weeds 16
bird's ear, white 70, *71*
birdseed (groundsel) 64, *65*
bishop weed 86, *87*
bittercress
   hairy 10, 12, 32, *33*
   New Zealand 32
   wavy 32
black heg 130, *131–3*
blackberry, wild 16, 126, 130, *131–3*
blackgrass 13
bluegrass, annual 13, 20, 60, *61*
bracken 108, *109*
brake fern 108, *109*
bud banks 8, 134
bulbils 8, 14, 134
bulbs 134
buttercup, creeping 6, 110, *111–13*

C

Caltha palustris 104
Calystegia sepium 92, *93*
calyx 134

Capsella bursa-pastoris 30, 31, 72
Cardamine concatenata 22
   C. corymbosa 32
   C. flexuosa 32
   C. hirsuta 32, *33*
catsear 120
causeway grass 60, *61*
celandine, lesser 104, *105*
Cerastium fontanum 70
Chamaemelum nobile 82
chamomile 82
Chenopodium album 34, *35*, 62
chicken weed (common chickweed) 70, *71*
chickenweed (groundsel) 64, *65*
chickweed, common 13, 28, 70, *71*
cinquefoil, creeping 110
Circaea lutetiana 66
Cirsium arvense 94, *95*
   C. vulgare 94
cleavers 10, 20, 44, *45*
clover 13, 16
cocklebur, rough 38
compass plant 48, *49*
contact weedkillers 134
Convolvulus arvensis 92
Conyza canadensis 36, *37*
   C. sumatrensis 36
corn speedwell 76, *77*
cotyledons *9*, 134
couch grass 13, 80, 96, *97*

cover crops 7, 134
cow parsley 6
cross-pollination 134
crowfoot, creeping 110, *111–13*
cultivation 134

D

daisy
    English 13, 52, 90, *91*
    ox-eye 90
dandelion 10, 80, 120, *121–3*
Datura stramonium 38, *39*
days-eye 90, *91*
dead-nettle
    henbit 50
    red 13, 20, 50, *51*
devil's snare 38, *39*
dewberry 130
dish mustard 72, *73*
dock 80
    broad-leaved 116, *117*
    common 116, *117*
    curled 116
dormancy, seeds 8, 20, 134

E

edible weeds 6
elephant ears 114, *115*
Elymus repens 96, *97*
ephemerals 20, 134
Epilobium 98, *99*
    E. angustifolium 98
    E. ciliatum 98
Equisetum arvense 100, *101–3*
    E. hyemale 100
ericaceous plants 134
Erigeron bonariensis 36
Euphorbia helioscopia 40
    E. peplus 40, *41*
explosive seed pods 10, 134

F

Fallopia baldschuanica 114
fallow ground 134
fertile seeds 134
Ficaria verna subsp. *verna*
    104, *105*
fireweed 98, *99*
fleabane
    Canadian 36, *37*, 98
    flax-leaf 36
    Guernsey 36
flickweed 32, *33*
floods, spreading seeds 10
flowers *9*
forget-me-not, field 52, *53*

G

Galinsoga parviflora 12,
    42, *43*
    G. quadriradiata 42
Galium aparine 44, *45*
gallant soldier 42 *43*
garlic
    crow 88
    wild 88, *89*
garlic mustard 22, 23
germination 8
Glechoma hederacea 76
goosefoot 34, *35*
goosegrass 44, *45*
goutweed 86, *87*
grain crops 13
green manures 7, 134
ground elder 6, 12, 13, 80,
    86, *87*
ground ivy 76
groundsel 10, 20, 64, *65*
Guizotia abyssinica 12

H

hairy bittercress 10, 12, 32, *33*
hand-weeding 7, 134
hawkbit 120
hedge bindweed 13, 80, 92, *93*

Heracleum mantegazzianum
    46
herbicides 6, 7, 134, 135
Himalayan balsam 12, 46, *47*
Hippuris vulgaris 100
hoeing 7, 10, 135
hogweed, giant 46
honeysuckle, Himalayan 114
horsetail 80, 100, *101–3*
horseweed 36, *37*
houndberry 66, *67*
Houttuynia cordata 114
Hypochaeris radicata 120
hypocotyl *9*

I

Impatiens glandulifera 46, *47*
insects, benefits of weeds 16
integrated weed management 7
international weed spread 10–12
invasive plant 7, 12
Irish moss 118, *119*
iron grass 62, 63
ivy chickweed 76, *77*
ivy-leaved speedwell 76, *77*

J

Jack-by-the-hedge 22, *23*
Japanese knotweed 10, 12, 46,
    80, 114, *115*
jimson weed 12, 38, *39*

K

Kew weed 42, *43*
kiss-over-the-garden-gate
    58, *59*
knotweed 62, *63*
knotweed, Japanese 10, 12, 46,
    80, 114, *115*

L

Lactuca serriola 48, *49*
    L. virosa 48
lamb's quarters 34, *35*

Lamium amplexicaule 50
   L. purpureum 50, *51*
lawns 7, 13, 16, 135
leaves *9*, 135
leek, three-cornered 88
Leontodon 120
lettuce
   greater 48
   prickly 48, *49*
Leucanthemum vulgare
   90
Leycesteria formosa 114
life cycles 13, 20
light, and germination 8
Lysichiton americanus 12

M

mare's tail 100, *101–3*
marsh marigold 104
Matricaria discoidea 82
milfoil 82, *83–5*
milk thistle 48, *49*, 68, *69*
milkweed 40, *41*
mouse-ear chickweed,
   common 70
mugwort 26
mulches 7, 10, 13, 135
mustard
   dish 72, *73*
   garlic 22, 23
Myosotis arvensis 52, 53

N

nettle 6, 13, 16, 80
   annual 74, *75*
   perennial 74
   small 74, *75*
niger seeds 12
nightshade
   black 66, *67*
   enchanter's 66
   garden 66, *67*
   woody 66
nitrates 13

no-dig gardening 135
nodes 135

O

one-o-clocks 120, *121–3*
orache, common 34
overwintering annuals 13, 20
oxalis, creeping 54, *55–7*
Oxalis corniculata 54, *55–7*
   O. debilis 54
   O. latifolia 54

P

pearlwort 118, *119*
pennycress, field 72, 73
perennial weeds 8, 13, 78–123,
   135
   benefits for wildlife 16
   management 14
   spreading 10
Persicaria 114
   P. lapathifolia 58
   P. maculosa 58, *59*
persicaria, pale 58
persicary 58, *59*
petty spurge 40, *41*
pilewort 104, *105*
pimpernel, scarlet 28, *29*
pineappleweed 82
Plantago major 106, *107*
plantain
   broadleaf 106, *107*
Poa annua 60, *61*
policeman's helmet 46, *47*
Polygonatum 114
Polygonum aviculare 62, 63
poor man's barometer 28, *29*
poppies 30
popping cress 32, *33*
Potentilla reptans 110
prickly lettuce 48, *49*
Pteridium aquilinum 108, *109*

Q

quackgrass 96, *97*

R

ragweed
   common 12, 26, *27*
   western 26
ragwort 6, 64, 94
ramsons 88, *89*
Ranunculus repens 110, *111–13*
red leg 58, *59*
Reynoutria japonica 114, *115*
rhizomes 8, *11*, 135
ribgrass 106, *107*
roots *9*
   perennial weeds 10, *11*, 14
Rubus caesius 130
   R. fruticosus 130, *131–3*
Rumex crispus 116
   R. obtusifolius 116, *117*
runners 135
Russian vine 114

S

Sagina procumbens 118, *119*
scarlet pimpernel 28, *29*
scorpion grass 52, *53*
seed banks 8, 135
seedlings *9*
seeds *11*, 135
   annual weeds 8
   benefits for wildlife 16
   dispersal 10–12
   dormancy 8, 20, 134
   germination 8
   international spread 10–12
   perennial weeds 10
   weed management 14
self-fertile plants 135
Senecio jacobaea 64, 94
   S. vulgaris 64, *65*
sepals 135
shaggy soldier 42
shepherd's purse 30, *31*, 72

skunk cabbage 12
smartweed 58, *59*
soilborne seeds 135
Solanum dulcamara 66
   S. nigrum 66, *67*
Sonchus arvensis 68
   S. asper 68
   S. oleraceus 68, *69*
sorrel
   creeping wood 54, 55–7
   wood 12
   yellow 54, 55–7
sowthistle
   common 68, *69*
   perennial 68
   prickly 68
speedwell 13, 44
   bird's-eye 76
   corn 76, *77*
   germander 76
   green field 76
   ivy-leaved 76, *77*
   slender 76
   thyme-leaved 76
spores 135
spurge
   petty 40, *41*
   sun 40
stale seedbeds 7, 10, 135
Stellaria media 70, *71*
sticky willy 44, *45*
stinkweed 72, *73*
stolons *11*, 135
sustainability 7
sycamore maple 126, 128, *129*
systemic weedkillers 135

T
Taraxacum 120, *121–3*
temperatures, and germination
   8
thistle 13
   Canada 94, *95*

common sowthistle 68, *69*
creeping 80, 94, *95*
milk thistle 68, *69*
prickly 94, *95*
spear 94
Thlaspi arvense 72, *73*
thorn apple 38, *39*
toothwort, cut-leaf 22
tree seedlings 126
trimming 7
true leaves 135
turf 135
twitch 96, *97*

U
Urtica dioica 74
   U. urens 74, *75*

V
vegetable gardens 13
Veronica agrestis 76
   V. arvensis 76
   V. chamaedrys 76
   V. filiformis 76
   V. hederifolia 76, *77*
   V. persica 76
   V. serpyllifolia 76

W
waterborne seeds 135
way bread 106, *107*
weed management 14
weedkillers 6, 7, 134, 135
weeds, definition 6–7
white goosefoot 13, 34, *35*, 62
wild plants 6
wildlife, benefits of weeds 7, 16
willow weed 58, *59*
willowherb 98, *99*
   fringed 98
   rosebay 98
wind-borne seeds 10, 135
winter-weed 76, *77*

wood sorrel, creeping 12, 54,
   55–7
woody weeds 124–35

X
Xanthium strumarium 38

Y
yarrow 82, *83–5*

Acknowledgments

Deep thanks to Chris Young, horticultural publishing consultant, for suggesting me as author, and Helen Griffin at the RHS for accepting his suggestion.

Sophie Blackman of DK for good-humored support while managing the process, and Diana Vowles for fitting my precious words to available space while retaining the full sense.

Neil Hepworth, freelance photographer, for making beautiful yet informative images of what might have been a rather mundane subject matter in other hands.

And finally, thanks to my colleagues at RHS gardens, in the RHS science team, and RHS libraries, for their tolerance and sharing their knowledge with me over many years. All mistakes, errors, and other infelicities, however, remain mine and mine alone.

Publisher acknowledgments

DK would like to thank Katie Hewett for the proofread, Hilary Bird for the index, Dawn Titmus for editorial assistance, Ashok Kumar and Vagisha Pushp for picture research, and Lori Hand for US consulting.

Picture credits

The publisher would like to thank the following for their kind permission to reproduce their photographs:

(Key: a-above; b-below/bottom; c-center; f-far; l-left; r-right; t-top)

27 Alamy Stock Photo: WILDLIFE GmbH (tl). **Dreamstime.com:** Sunlikegraphics (r). **Getty Images/iStock:** OlyaSolodenko (cl). **29 Dreamstime.com:** Bhupinder Kaur (tr); Christopher Smith (l). **33 Alamy Stock Photo:** imageBROKER.com GmbH & Co. KG/Nigel Cattlin (tl). **RHS:** Barry Phillips (b). **35 Alamy Stock Photo:** Marcus Harrison—plants (cr). **37 Dreamstime.com:** Mykola Ohorodnyk (r). **39 Alamy Stock Photo:** Nigel Cattlin (tl); Satriady Utomo (tr); Guido Paradisi (bl). **45 Alamy Stock Photo:** Nigel Cattlin (tl). **47 Alamy Stock Photo:** blickwinkel/A. Jagel (tl). **Dreamstime.com:** Lontano (bl). **49 Alamy Stock Photo:** blickwinkel (b); Design Pics Inc/Joe DiTomaso/AgStock—RF (tl). **Getty Images/iStock:** Santi Wiwatchaikul (tr). **51 Dreamstime.com:** Miroslav Hlavko (cl). **Shutterstock.com:** NataFrank (r). **53 Alamy Stock Photo:** Nigel Cattlin (bl). **67 RHS:** Barry Phillips (b). **69 Alamy Stock Photo:** Laura Primo (cl). **73 Alamy Stock Photo:** Nigel Cattlin (tl); Zoonar GmbH/Joerg Hemmer (cl). **Dreamstime.com:** Orest Lyzhechka (r). **77 Alamy Stock Photo:** AGAMI Photo Agency/Wil Leurs (cl); Nigel Cattlin (tl). **89 Alamy Stock Photo:** Panther Media GmbH/emer (tr); rdonar (tl). **Marianne Majerus Garden Images:** (b). **95 Alamy Stock Photo:** Nigel Cattlin (tl); Elizabeth Wake (tr). **Shutterstock.com:** AS Foodstudio (b). **105 Alamy Stock Photo:** blickwinkel/Koenig (cl). **Dreamstime.com:** Viktoria Ivanets (tl). **naturepl.com:** Linda Pitkin (r). **111 Alamy Stock Photo:** Nigel Cattlin (tl). **115 Alamy Stock Photo:** blickwinkel/G. Czepluch (b). **Getty Images/iStock:** Kicocollection (tl). **117 Alamy Stock Photo:** Nigel Cattlin (tl). **119 Alamy Stock Photo:** blickwinkel/F. Hecker (tl); Keith Burdett (r)

All other images © Dorling Kindersley

DK LONDON
Editorial Manager Ruth O'Rourke
Senior Editor Sophie Blackman
Senior Designer Barbara Zuniga
Senior US Editor Megan Douglass
Production Editor David Almond
Senior Production Controller Stephanie McConnell
Jacket Designer Izzy Poulson
DTP and Design Co-ordinator Heather Blagden
Sales Material Co-ordinator Emily Cannings
Art Director Maxine Pedliham
Publishing Director Katie Cowan

Editorial Diana Vowles
Photography Neil Hepworth
Consultant Gardening Publisher Chris Young

DK DELHI
Editor Ankita Gupta
Managing Editor Saloni Singh
Managing Art Editor Neha Ahuja Chowdhry
Senior Picture Researcher Aditya Katyal
DTP Designers Manish Upreti, Rajdeep Singh
DTP Coordinator Pushpak Tyagi
Pre-production Manager Balwant Singh
Production Manager Pankaj Sharma
Creative Head Ma avika Talukder

ROYAL HORTICULTURAL SOCIETY
Consultant Simon Maughan
RHS Books Publishing Manager Helen Griffin

First American Edition, 2024
Published in the United States by DK Publishing
1745 Broadway, 20th Floor, New York, NY 10019

A catalog record for this book
is available from the Library of Congress.
ISBN: 978-0-7440-9237-0

Printed and bound in China

www.dk.com